1-2-3
FOR
DUMMIES™
Quick Reference

by John Walkenbach
Preface by Series Editor Dan Gookin

IDG
BOOKS

IDG Books Worldwide, Inc.
An International Data Group Company

San Mateo, California ♦ Indianapolis, Indiana ♦ Boston, Massachusetts

1-2-3 For Dummies Quick Reference

Published by
IDG Books Worldwide, Inc.
An International Data Group Company
155 Bovet Road, Suite 310
San Mateo, CA 94402

Library of Congress Catalog Card No.:93-78448

ISBN 1-56884-027-6

Printed in the United States of America

10 9 8 7 6 5 4 3 2 1

Distributed in the United States by IDG Books Worldwide, Inc.

Distributed in Canada by Macmillan of Canada, a Division of
Canada Publishing Corporation; by Woodslane Pty. Ltd. in Austra-
lia and New Zealand; and by Computer Bookshops in the U.K. and
Ireland.

For information on translations and availability in other countries,
contact Marc Jeffrey Mikulich, Foreign Rights Manager, at IDG
Books Worldwide; FAX NUMBER 415-358-1260.

For sales inquiries and special prices for bulk quantities, write to
the address above or call IDG Books Worldwide at 415-312-0650.

COMPUTER
BOOK SERIES
FROM IDG

is a trademark of IDG Books Worldwide, Inc.

Acknowledgments

Thanks to everyone who helped out on this project — all the folks at IDG Books, especially Janna Custer (the Acquisitions Editor who chose me for the project) and Diane Steele and Sara Black (who edited my ramblings so normal people could understand them). Thanks are also due to the great IDG Books production staff and all the others who pretty much remain behind the scenes. They're the ones who turned my Word for Windows files into a real book. I also appreciate the thorough technical review by Bob Garza, who set me straight on a few things while I was lost in the 1-2-3 menu tree. Thanks are also due to Dan Gookin, the guy who came up with the original concept for these ...*For Dummies* books. Maybe some day we'll meet. And finally, I wish to acknowledge VaRene (she knows why).

John Walkenbach
La Jolla, California

(The publisher would like to give special thanks to Patrick J. McGovern, without whom this book would not have been possible.)

Credits

Publisher
David Solomon

Acquisitions Editor
Janna Custer

Managing Editor
Mary Bednarek

Project Editor
Diane Graves Steele

Editors
Sara Black
Kezia Endsley

Technical Reviewer
Victor R. Garza

Production Manager
Beth J. Baker

Production Coordinator
Cindy L. Phipps

Production Staff
Joseph A. Augsburger
Mary Breidenbach
Drew R. Moore

Indexer
Sherry Massey

A Call to Readers:

We want to Hear From You!

Listen up, all you readers of IDG's *1-2-3 For Dummies Quick Reference.*It is time for you to take advantage of a new, direct pipeline for readers of IDG's international bestsellers — the famous . . . *For Dummies* books.

We would like your input for future printings and editions of this book. Tell us what you liked (and didn't like) about the *1-2-3 For Dummies Quick Reference.*

We'll add you to our *Dummies Database/Fan Club* and keep you up to date on the latest . . . *For Dummies* books, news, cartoons, calendars, and more!

Please send your name, address, and phone number, as well as your comments, questions, and suggestions, to:

. . . For Dummies Coordinator
IDG Books Worldwide
3250 North Post Road, Suite 140
Indianapolis, Indiana 46226

Thanks for your input!

About the Author

John Walkenbach, the guy who pulled this together, has used
1-2-3 since it was first released. He's a contributing editor for *PC
World* and *InfoWorld,* co-author of the *PC World 1-2-3 for Windows
Complete Handbook* and the *PC World Excel for Windows Handbook,* and author of *Quattro Pro For Dummies* and *Developing
Applications with Quattro Pro for Windows.* He holds a Ph.D. in
experimental psychology from the University of Montana and has
worked as an instructor, programmer, consultant, and market
researcher in the banking industry. When he's not writing about
computers, he's probably playing around in his MIDI studio,
working on his latest music-oriented shareware creation or
annoying his neighbors with weird synthetic sounds.

About the Series Editor

Dan Gookin, the author of *DOS For Dummies, DOS For Dummies,
2nd Edition, WordPerfect For Dummies, WordPerfect 6 For
Dummies,* and co-author of *PCs For Dummies* and the *Illustrated
Computer Dictionary For Dummies,* is a writer and computer
"guru" whose job is to remind everyone that computers are not to
be taken too seriously. Presently, Mr. Gookin works for himself as
a freelance writer. Gookin holds a degree in Communications
from the University of California, San Diego, and is a regular
contributor to *InfoWorld, PC/Computing, DOS Resource Guide,* and
PC Buying World magazines.

About IDG Books Worldwide

Welcome to the world of IDG Books Worldwide.

IDG Books Worldwide, Inc., is a division of International Data Group, the world's largest publisher of computer-related information and the leading global provider of information services on information technology. IDG publishes over 194 computer publications in 62 countries. Forty million people read one or more IDG publications each month.

If you use personal computers, IDG Books is committed to publishing quality books that meet your needs. We rely on our extensive network of publications, including such leading periodicals as *Macworld, InfoWorld, PC World, Publish, Computerworld, Network World*, and *SunWorld*, to help us make informed and timely decisions in creating useful computer books that meet your needs.

Every IDG book strives to bring extra value and skill-building instruction to the reader. Our books are written by experts, with the backing of IDG periodicals, and with careful thought devoted to issues such as audience, interior design, use of icons, and illustrations. Our editorial staff is a careful mix of high-tech journalists and experienced book people. Our close contact with the makers of computer products helps ensure accuracy and thorough coverage. Our heavy use of personal computers at every step in production means we can deliver books in the most timely manner.

We are delivering books of high quality at competitive prices on topics customers want. At IDG, we believe in quality, and we have been delivering quality for over 25 years. You'll find no better book on a subject than an IDG book.

> John Kilcullen
> President and C.E.O.
> IDG Books Worldwide, Inc.

IDG Books Worldwide, Inc. is a division of International Data Group. The officers are Patrick J. McGovern, Founder and Board Chairman; Walter Boyd, President. International Data Group's publications include: **ARGENTINA's** Computerworld Argentina, InfoWorld Argentina; **ASIA's** Computerworld Hong Kong, PC World Hong Kong, Computerworld Southeast Asia, PC World Singapore, Computerworld Malaysia, PC World Malaysia; **AUSTRALIA's** Computerworld Australia, Australian PC World, Australian Macworld, Network World, Reseller, IDG Sources; **AUSTRIA's** Computerwelt Oesterreich, PC Test; **BRAZIL's** Computerworld, Mundo IBM, Mundo Unix, PC World, Publish; **BULGARIA's** Computerworld Bulgaria, Ediworld, PC & Mac World Bulgaria; **CANADA's** Direct Access, Graduate Computerworld, InfoCanada, Network World Canada; **CHILE's** Computerworld, Informatica; **COLUMBIA's** Computerworld Columbia; **CZECH REPUBLIC's** Computerworld, Elektronika, PC World; **DENMARK's** CAD/CAM WORLD, Communications World, Computerworld Danmark, LOTUS World, Macintosh Produktkatalog, Macworld Danmark, PC World Danmark, PC World Produktguide, Windows World; **EQUADOR's** PC World; **EGYPT's** Computerworld (CW) Middle East, PC World Middle East; **FINLAND's** MikroPC, Tietoviikko, Tietoverkko; **FRANCE's** Distributique, GOLDEN MAC, InfoPC, Languages & Systems, Le Guide du Monde Informatique, Le Monde Informatique, Telecoms & Reseaux; **GERMANY's** Computerwoche, Computerwoche Focus, Computerwoche Extra, Computerwoche Karriere, Information Management, Macwelt, Netzwelt, PC Welt, PC Woche, Publish, Unit; **HUNGARY's** Alaplap, Computerworld SZT, PC World, ; **INDIA's** Computers & Communications; **ISRAEL's** Computerworld Israel, PC World Israel; **ITALY's** Computerworld Italia, Lotus Magazine, Macworld Italia, Networking Italia, PC World Italia; **JAPAN's** Computerworld Japan, Macworld Japan, SunWorld Japan, Windows World; **KENYA's** East African Computer News; **KOREA's** Computerworld Korea, Macworld Korea, PC World Korea; **MEXICO's** Compu Edicion, Compu Manufactura, Computacion/Punto de Venta, Computerworld Mexico, MacWorld, Mundo Unix, PC World, Windows; **THE NETHERLAND'S** Computer! Totaal, LAN Magazine, MacWorld; **NEW ZEALAND's** Computer Listings, Computerworld New Zealand, New Zealand PC World; **NIGERIA's** PC World Africa; **NORWAY's** Computerworld Norge, C/World, Lotusworld Norge, Macworld Norge, Networld, PC World Ekspress, PC World Norge, PC World's Product Guide, Publish World, Student Data, Unix World, Windowsworld, IDG Direct Response; **PANAMA's** PC World; **PERU's** Computerworld Peru, PC World; **PEOPLES REPUBLIC OF CHINA's** China Computerworld, PC World China, Electronics International, China Network World; **IDG HIGH TECH BEIJING's** New Product World; **IDG SHENZHEN's** Computer News Digest; **PHILLIPINES'** Computerworld, PC World; **POLAND's** Computerworld Poland, PC World/ Komputer; **PORTUGAL's** Cerebro/PC World, Correio Informatico/Computerworld, MacIn; **ROMANIA's** PC World; **RUSSIA's** Computerworld-Moscow, Mir-PC, Sety; **SLOVENIA's** Monitor Magazine; **SOUTH AFRICA's** Computing S.A.; **SPAIN's** Amiga World, Computerworld Espana, Communicaciones World, Macworld Espana, NeXTWORLD, PC World Espana, Publish, Sunworld; **SWEDEN's** Attack, ComputerSweden, Corporate Computing, Lokala Natverk/LAN, Lotus World, MAC&PC, Macworld, Mikrodatorn, PC World, Publishing & Design (CAP), Datalngenjoren, Maxi Data, Windows World; **SWITZERLAND's** Computerworld Schweiz, Macworld Schweiz, PC & Workstation; **TAIWAN's** Computerworld Taiwan, Global Computer Express, PC World Taiwan; **THAILAND's** Thai Computerworld; **TURKEY's** Computerworld Monitor, Macworld Turkiye, PC World Turkiye; **UNITED KINGDOM's** Lotus Magazine, Macworld, Sunworld; **UNITED STATES'** AmigaWorld, Cable in the Classroom, CD Review, CIO, Computerworld, Desktop Video World, DOS Resource Guide, Electronic News, Federal Computer Week, Federal Integrator, GamePro, IDG Books, InfoWorld, InfoWorld Direct, Laser Event, Macworld, Multimedia World, Network World, NeXTWORLD, PC Games, PC Letter, PC World Publish, Sumeria, SunWorld, SWATPro, Video Event; **VENEZUELA's** Computerworld Venezuela, MicroComputerworld Venezuela; **VIETNAM's** PC World Vietnam

Contents at a Glance

Preface

DOS For Dummies — and all the books in the *...For Dummies* series — are the ideal computer references. Have a problem? Great, look it up in *...For Dummies,* find out how to get it done right, and then close the book and return to your work. That's the way all computer books should work: quickly, painlessly, and with a dash of humor to keep the edge off.

So why is a 1-2-3 quick reference needed? Yikes! Who wants to look at that junk? Who cares about the /SPITOON or the :WAMBOOLI command? Chances are you might, someday.

The way we work with computers is that we often imitate what others do. Fred may hand you a spreadsheet file and say, "Recalculate these formulas before you quit work today." Being suspicious—which is always good around Fred—you want to make sure you won't be doing anything disastrous. *1-2-3 For Dummies* can't help you weasel out command formats and, seldom-used options on commands that are way beyond the reach of the typical Dummy. So what you're left with is the 1-2-3 manual or the fuzzy-headed online help.

Thank goodness for this book!

John Walkenbach has done the tedious job of transposing all the 1-2-3 commands from crypto-manual speak into a plain language reference we can use during those painful "must look it up in the manual" moments. He's peppered it with information, dos and don'ts, and the splash of humor you've come to expect from any book with *Dummies* on the title.

So tuck this reference in tight somewhere right by your PC. Keep it handy for when you must know the advanced options of some command or to confirm your worst fears about what it is Fred wants you to do to your own PC.

Dan Gookin

Introduction

What! Another 1-2-3 Book?

Lotus 1-2-3 is the biggest selling computer software application in the history of the world — perhaps even the universe. In other words, millions of people around the world have this program installed on their PCs, and hundreds more are shelling out real money every day for a copy of this program. And it's a safe bet that the majority of these folks don't have a clue as to what the program can really do.

Practically every 1-2-3 user eventually reaches a head-scratching point in which they want to do something but cannot figure out where the command is located. Others just can't seem to get a command to do what they think it *should* do.

When I was asked to write this book, I visited a few local book stores to get an idea of what was out there. Literally hundreds of 1-2-3 books have been written. With a few exceptions, these books are dull, boring, and not much fun to read. An exception to the rule is Greg Harvey's *1-2-3 For Dummies.* Because of its light-hearted approach to teaching about computers and software, the *...For Dummies* series is the most popular computer book series ever. This book follows in the same vein and was written as a companion to *1-2-3 For Dummies.*

Important Note: This book covers 1-2-3 Release 2.4. Although it is of some value to 1-2-3 Release 3.x users and 1-2-3 for Windows users, it does not cover all the commands available in these more advanced versions.

Slashing Around

Some day, computers will be able to respond to your vocal commands. You could say something like, "Hey computer, run 1-2-3 and load that file I was working on Thursday afternoon. Then change the interest rate cell to 8.5%. Thanks, dude." Until that day arrives, you're going to have to give commands in a way that the computer can understand.

If you have used 1-2-3 for even a few minutes, you undoubtedly know that the / (slash) key opens the door to a staggering number of commands by displaying the 1-2-3 menu. You can change how your numbers look, move stuff around, print your work, and even invert a matrix.

Believe it or not, thousands of people have memorized virtually every command sequence available in 1-2-3. Ask them how to make the time of day display at the bottom of the screen, and they reply, "Slash Worksheet Global Default Other Clock Clock," without even batting an eye. If they're in a hurry, they simply say, "Slash WGDOCC." You can easily identify these people by their pocket protectors which sport the 1-2-3 logo. Most people, though, memorize only the commands that are *important* (and they don't wear pocket protectors).

To Slash, to Highlight, to Click — It's User's Choice

Here's a typical 1-2-3 command: /**R**ange **F**ormat. You can summon this command in three different ways.

- Type /**RF** (the first letter of each word).

- Press the / (slash) key to activate the menu; use the arrow keys to highlight the Range menu and press Enter; then use the arrow keys to highlight the Format menu and press Enter. This procedure takes more keystrokes than typing /**RF**.

- If you have a mouse, move the mouse pointer to the menu bar area to make the menu appear; then click on Range and click on Format.

After you invoke the command, it displays a submenu with a list of choices for formatting. Choose one of these options by using the first letter, the arrow keys and Enter, or a mouse click.

For some commands you then need to respond to one or more additional menus. It's easy to get lost in the menu maze. Fortunately, 1-2-3 sometimes shows you setting sheets that let you see all the settings and change them in the setting sheet window (and avoid the menus). An example of a setting sheet is the screen that pops up when you invoke the /**G**raph command.

By the way, many SmartIcons are available for mouse users. Over the course of a few years, the SmartIcons may save you as much as an hour or two. The real advantage to using SmartIcons is that it's easier than fiddling with the menus. But not all commands have equivalent SmartIcons — and, of course, you have to know what all the icons do. Part VII is a good place to learn about SmartIcons.

How the 1-2-3 Commands Look in This Book

This reference guide is all about the 1-2-3 commands, so we need to be on the same wavelength, that is, you need to know where my head was when I was writing this book.

Here's an example using the /Range Format command. This particular command makes the values in a range of cells take on a different numerical format. When I talk about this command in the book, it appears in the heading as

/Range Format

The icons that appear with each command name tell you at a glance something about the command — how often you are likely to use it and how safe it is for you to use.

Then each command gets a brief English-language description of what it does. I tell you why you would ever want (or need) to use this command. When you issue most commands, you cannot simply stop there. You need to go "deeper" into the menu to tell 1-2-3 exactly what you're trying to do. Therefore, for each main command, I tell you what all the subcommands under it do.

If the command is one that I have determined to be particularly troublesome or hard to use, I give you instructions to help clarify things. And if there's anything else you should know about, I tell you. Finally, I refer you to other commands that may be of interest — one of them could be the one that you *really* want to use.

Parts IV, V, VI, and VII are organized in tables to give you easy access to the information they offer you.

What the Little Pictures Mean

This book uses icons liberally. These icons tell you in an instant a few key things about each command. Here's what they mean:

 This icon flags commands that are used by almost all 1-2-3 users. It's probably worth your while to learn about these commands.

 This icon flags commands that are used only by advanced 1-2-3 users or for special purposes. These commands can be useful at times.

 This icon flags commands that are hardly ever used.

Safe for your data.

Generally safe in most circumstances unless you really don't follow instructions, then look out.

Potentially dangerous to data but necessary in the scheme of things. Be very careful when you use this command!

This icon flags areas that can cause problems if you're not careful.

Look out! There's some little something in this command that can get you into trouble (even when it's rated safe or generally safe).

This icon flags information that may not be immediately obvious to you. It might be another way of using a command or general hint that will make using 1-2-3 a snap.

This icon flags material that tells you where to look in *1-2-3 For Dummies* for more information. If you don't have *1-2-3 For Dummies,* go out and buy it so you can use this stuff!

This icon flags cross references to other places in this book that might give you some more help.

How I Organized This Book

This book has seven Parts.

Part I: A Crash Course in 1-2-3. This section is a quick and dirty overview of 1-2-3 basics. I was tempted to leave out this information and simply refer you to *1-2-3 For Dummies,* but I'm a nice guy.

Part II: The 1-2-3 Command Reference. Here's the heart of the book, as it were. It's an alphabetical listing of all the menu commands, with just enough detail to get you working again when you're stuck.

Part III: The Wysiwyg Command Reference. If Part II qualifies as the heart of the book, this one's more like the liver. If you use the Wysiwyg add-in (which gives you fancy formatting), you need all the commands in this section.

Part IV: The Dummy's Guide to @Functions. This section explains all these weird — but sometimes useful — @functions in simple language.

Part V: The Dummy's Guide to Macro Commands. Although most 1-2-3 users don't create macros, I include this section so that no one will write in and ask how I can possibly call this a reference guide if it doesn't cover macro commands. Look at it this way: if you're ever forced to learn macros, you do not have to buy another reference guide.

Part VI: The Dummy's Guide to 1-2-3 Keys. What happens if I press this key? Here's the place to find the answer.

Part VII: The Dummy's Guide to 1-2-3 SmartIcons. If you have a mouse, you can save yourself many trips to the 1-2-3 menu by learning what all those SmartIcons do and prevent wear and tear on your / (slash) key.

How You Can Use This Book

You can use this book in several ways.

- If you need to find out how to do something, look up the main menu command (commands are in alphabetical order in each Part, not the order in which they appear on-screen). Browse through that discussion until you find something that looks relevant and then read it.

- If you don't have a clue as to the proper command to look up, go to the index. This tactic usually steers you to the command that you're looking for.

- If you need to find out why something isn't working the way you think it should, look up the command and read about it. I've thrown in all sorts of useful tips and techniques — at no extra charge.

- If you find yourself with a spare hour or two while circling over LAX waiting to land, browse through the book and read stuff that interests you.

- Keep it lying around on your desk. That way, people walking by will stop and make idle conversation while trying to get a look at the book without actually telling you they need the help! It's a good way to kill some time when you should be working.

Part 1:
A Crash Course in 1-2-3

For those of you who didn't buy *1-2-3 For Dummies*, here's a condensed version (without all the good jokes and cartoons). You can read through this section to get a quick overview of 1-2-3 or use it to refresh your 1-2-3 memory.

Basic 1-2-3 Knowledge

1-2-3 is one of several products in a class of application software programs called *spreadsheets*. Spreadsheets work with *spreadsheet files* (also known as *worksheets* because a spreadsheet program is an electronic version of an accountant's green worksheet). A spreadsheet file is made up of cells. Each cell can hold a number, a label (text), a formula, or nothing at all. You can also create graphs from the numbers stored in a spreadsheet file.

People use spreadsheets for many things, but most of them involve numerical calculations. The real beauty of a spreadsheet lies in the formulas. Formulas usually refer to other cells that contain numbers or other formulas. When you change anything in any cell, all the formulas recalculate to show new answers based on the current *values* (numbers that stand for quantities, dates, times, or formulas) in cells.

If you're just starting out with 1-2-3, I strongly urge you to read *1-2-3 For Dummies*. That book tells you everything you need to know about starting the program and getting up to speed.

Navigational Techniques

A spreadsheet file is fairly huge. In fact, each file has 256 columns and 8,192 rows. Rows are identified by actual numbers, but columns use letters. After column Z comes column AA, which is followed by AB, and so on. After column AA comes BA — well, you get the picture.

A *cell* is the intersection of a row and a column. Therefore, a spreadsheet has 2,097,152 cells (I used 1-2-3 to calculate that number). If you were to fill every cell with a number (which you cannot actually do, so don't try it) and print it, the printout would be about 21 feet wide and 171 feet long — even bigger if you used large type.

Because you cannot see the entire spreadsheet at once, you have to scroll though it using the keyboard. Things work pretty much the way you might expect: the arrow keys move around one cell at a time, and PgUp and PgDn move you up and down one screenful at a time.

At any given time, one of the 2 million or so cells is the *active cell*. The active cell is the one that contains the *cell pointer*. You can tell the cell pointer because it's a different color than the others, and it moves when you press the arrow keys.

The 1-2-3 Screen

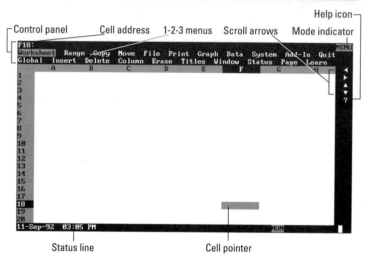

Figure 1: The anatomy of a blank 1-2-3 screen.

Besides showing cells, the 1-2-3 screen is filled with lots of other information. The official name for the first three lines is the *control panel.* The first line of the control panel tells you about the current cell (the one with the cell pointer) and also what *mode* you're in (when you're in READY mode, you can enter things in cells). The second control panel line shows the menu commands. These menus appear like magic whenever you press the / (slash) key or move your mouse into this area. The last line in the control panel shows the subcommands for the highlighted command in the top line of the menu.

The bottom line of the 1-2-3 screen goes by the name *status line.* As you might expect, this line tells you about the status of certain things, such as whether you have the Num Lock key on. It can also show the date and time — handy if your Rolex is at the cleaners.

The last few columns of the 1-2-3 screen are dedicated to mouse users. These columns contain little *scroll arrow icons* that make moving around in the worksheet easier if you have a mouse. Why hunt and peck your way around the keyboard when you can click a mouse button and move the cell pointer in the direction that the arrow is pointing?

The last icon, the question mark, is the Help icon. Click on it any time to get the 1-2-3 Main Help Index if you need help and you can't find this book.

Data Entry

As I already mentioned, a cell can hold a number, a label, a formula, or nothing at all. To put something in a cell, 1-2-3 must be in READY mode. If the mode indicator doesn't say READY, keep pressing Escape until it does. If you want to put a number in a cell, just type the number and press Enter when you're done. Then use the direction keys to move to another cell and enter another number.

To put text in a cell, just type the text and press Enter when you're done. You can put a lot of text in a cell. If the cell to the right is empty, the text will "spill over" into it. If the neighboring cell is not empty, the extra text will get cut off on-screen (it's all there, it just doesn't show). If you're entering text and it starts with a number, you have to type a single quote character (') first. If you want to know why, you just have to buy *1-2-3 For Dummies* (see Chapter 2).

Entering formulas is another story. Usually, formulas refer to other cells in the worksheet and use the values in those cells. Here's a simple formula:

```
(+A1+A2)/2
```

This formula adds the values in cells A1 and A2 and divides the result by 2. Cells A1 and A2 can hold either numbers or other formulas. If either of these cells has a label (remember, that's text), 1-2-3 interprets it as zero. Whenever either cell A1 or A2 changes, the formula displays a new answer. This automatic recalculation of formulas is what makes spreadsheets so useful. Otherwise, they would simply be word processors set up with rows and columns.

Mousing Around with SmartIcons

If your system has a mouse attached, you may enjoy using the mouse with 1-2-3. But then again, you may find that sticking with the keyboard is more efficient. It's all a matter of what you're used to.

Chapter 11 in *1-2-3 For Dummies* tells you everything you would ever want to know about SmartIcons. You can also refer to Part 7 of this book for a handy SmartIcon reference.

Wysiwyg Mode

Back in the old days, 1-2-3 — like most other software — was strictly a text-based program: the screen displayed only text, usually 25 lines of 80 characters each. But a few years ago, Lotus began shipping an add-in called *Wysiwyg*. Wysiwyg lets you work with 1-2-3 in graphics mode so that *w*hat *y*ou *see* *is* *w*hat *y*ou *get*. The advantages with using Wysiwyg are that you can use different fonts and colors, draw fancy borders, stick graphs right next to your data, and otherwise impress your coworkers.

You can either use Wysiwyg or not. Using it takes up quite a bit of memory, so you may not be able to work with large files if you use Wysiwyg. And here's another hitch: Wysiwyg has its own set of menus in addition to the normal 1-2-3 menus. Pressing the / (slash) key calls up the normal menus, and pressing the : (colon) key calls up the Wysiwyg menus. Even worse, these menus usually don't communicate with each other.

If you're a relative beginner, you can make learning easy on yourself by ignoring Wysiwyg until you get more familiar with 1-2-3. With Wysiwyg, you've got about twice as many commands to deal with.

Doing Things

To accomplish anything significant in 1-2-3, you have to use the commands available on the menus. And that, my friend, is what the rest of this book is all about.

If this section whizzed by too fast for you, you're a good candidate for *1-2-3 For Dummies*. Part I, "The Absolute Basics," in that book covers all this essential information (and much more) in just a little more detail.

Part II:
The 1-2-3
Command Reference

OK folks, here's the good stuff, the reason you laid your good money on the counter for this information-packed little book. The following pages explain every single 1-2-3 command that you can possibly use. I admit that I provide longer explanations for the more commonly used commands, but if you're ever held at gun point and forced to do a data regression, you can rest assured that you'll find what it's all about by venturing no farther than the book you now hold in your hands.

Pay attention to all the icons described in the Introduction. These little pictures tell you, at a glance, important things about each command.

/Add-In Commands

The bigwigs at Lotus are pretty smart when it comes to 1-2-3. The program has been around for about a decade and still works much like the original version. However, the latest version has many new features that users have been begging for. Rather than add all these new features into the program, the Lotus people programmed 1-2-3 so that it can accept *add-in programs*. These programs let 1-2-3 do many interesting and useful things.

You can make your copy of 1-2-3 do more things by attaching one or more add-ins (and you can even set it up so that add-ins are loaded automatically whenever you run 1-2-3). You can then *invoke* these add-ins when you need them and *unload* them when you no longer need them. The real beauty of add-ins is that you don't have to load them if you don't want them. That way, you don't give up precious computer memory for things that you do not plan to use.

The most popular add-in is Wysiwyg; it comes with 1-2-3. Your system may be set up so that Wysiwyg is attached automatically. 1-2-3 includes six other add-ins, and you can buy even more from other software companies. The following table summarizes the add-ins that you already have and may not even know about.

Add-In Filename	*What It Does*
AUDITOR.ADN	Helps you locate errors in your worksheet.
BSOLVER.ADN	Tells you what value a cell needs to be to get the result you want in a formula.
ICONS.ADN	Makes the SmartIcons appear on the right of the screen. See Chapter 11 of *1-2-3 For Dummies* for more info.
MACROMGR.ADN	Lets macro mavens work with macro libraries. See Chapter 9 in *1-2-3 For Dummies* for more dirt on this.
TUTOR.ADN	Introduces 1-2-3 and provides an overview right on your computer.
VIEWER.ADN	Lets you look at worksheets on disk and even lets you set up a link to their cells. Chapter 4 in *1-2-3 For Dummies* tells you more.
WYSIWYG.ADN	Lets you do all sorts of fancy formatting on your worksheet. Chapter 10 in *1-2-3 For Dummies* is devoted to this topic.

With that introduction out of the way, let's move on to some commands.

/Add-In Attach

Attaches an add-in to 1-2-3 to let it do things that it normally cannot do.

Use the arrow keys to highlight the add-in you want and press Enter. Choose either **7**, **8**, **9**, or **10**. These numbers correspond to an Alt key combination that invokes the add-in; Alt-7 calls up the first add-in, for example. If you choose **No**-Key, you must invoke the add-in using the /**Add-In I**nvoke command. The Wysiwyg add-in doesn't need a key — you call it up by pressing **:** (colon).

More stuff

Some add-ins use up lots of memory, which takes away from the size of the worksheet you can have. It's usually not a good idea to load an add-in unless you absolutely need it. Otherwise, you're simply wasting valuable memory. And memory is a terrible thing to waste.

/**W**orksheet **G**lobal **D**efault **O**ther **A**dd-In **S**et

You can find more information on this command in Chapter 10 of *1-2-3 For Dummies*.

/Add-In Clear

Removes all add-ins from memory.

More stuff

Add-ins use up lots of memory, so if you ever get the dreaded Memory Full error, the first thing you should do is detach any add-ins that you don't absolutely need.

/**A**dd-In **D**etach

/Add-In Detach

Removes a specific add-in from memory.

 /**A**dd-In **C**lear

/Add-In Invoke

Starts (or invokes) an add-in that's already loaded into memory.

More stuff

If you need more memory for your worksheet or want to load another add-in, you can zap an add-in that you no longer need.

You need this command only if you didn't assign an Alt key combination to an add-in that you loaded.

/**A**dd-In **A**ttach

/Copy

Copies a single cell or a range from one location to another. Use this command if you want to make an exact copy of a range and don't feel like retyping it. Also use this command to copy a formula (or range of formulas) from one location to another.

To use this command, move the cell pointer to the *source* (the cell the holds the range or formula you want to copy), press Enter, move the cell pointer to the spot where you want to copy it (the *destination*), and press Enter.

More stuff

If you are copying to a range, highlight the range by pressing the period (.) to enter pointing mode and moving the cell pointer down to the last cell in the range.

Surveys show that this is one of the most popular and commonly used 1-2-3 commands ever. So if you use it, you're not alone.

Unlike most of the other menu commands, the /Copy command doesn't have any submenus.

When you copy formulas, the relative cell references change. If you copy a formula from Column A that reads *@SUM(A1..A10)* to Column B, the copied formula reads *@SUM(B1..B10)*. When you copy a whole range, you need to specify only the upper left cell for the destination range.

The /Copy command also copies formats and cell protection attributes. Suppose that you have a cell that's formatted to show up as currency. When you copy that cell, all its copies show up as currency, too.

The /Copy command is very useful, but it can also be destructive. When you copy something, the copy replaces what's already in the destination cell(s). And 1-2-3 doesn't bother to tell you that you're about to overwrite something that might be important.

/Move
:Special Copy

You can find more information on this command in Chapter 2 of *1-2-3 For Dummies*.

/Data Commands

Perform myriad duties that involve manipulation of ranges. For example, some of these commands let you work with data that's stored as a database: each row serves as a *record* and has several *fields,* which are the columns. But you don't need to know what a database is to use many of these commands.

/Data Distribution

Creates a frequency distribution of the values in a range. This command can be pretty useful: it tells you how many values in a range fall between 1 and 5, between 6 and 10, and so on. It can also tell you how many 1s, how many 2s, and so on, are in the range.

When you use this command, 1-2-3 prompts you for two things:

The *values range* lets you specify the range that holds the stuff that you want to count; enter the range.

The *bin range* lets you specify the range that holds the bins (the cutoffs); enter the range.

After you answer these prompts, press Enter and 1-2-3 puts the distribution directly to the right of the bin range.

More stuff

This command actually counts the number of values that fall between each of the bin values. In other words, the command also works if your values aren't whole numbers. For example, a value such as 3.2 would be counted in the 4 bin because it falls between 3 and 4 and is greater than 3.

You can also calculate frequency distributions using a bunch of @COUNT database @functions. You have to set up your data as a database and define a separate Criteria range for each bin. This process is harder to set up, but it has an advantage: the frequencies get updated automatically if your data changes.

If any of your data change, you have to issue the /Data **D**istribution command again. Well, you don't *have* to reissue it, but you can no longer trust the results of the command.

/Data Fill

Automatically puts a series of numbers into a range that you specify. You control the starting point, ending point, and the step between each number.

When you use this command, 1-2-3 prompts you for four things:

Fill range tells 1-2-3 where you want the numbers to go; enter the range.

Start specifies the starting value of the series; enter the number.

Step specifies the value that you want to increment each number in the series by. For example, if you want a series like 1, 3, 5,..., enter a Step Value of 2. (This value also can be negative, but if it is, make sure that your Stop value is smaller than your Start Number.) Enter the number.

Stop specifies the ending point. Any value that's larger than the final number in the range works just fine (it defaults to 8191). Enter the number.

Press Enter and 1-2-3 goes to work and fills in the series per your instructions.

More stuff

This command also works with dates and times.

This command is mainly a time-saver — a fast way to fill in a large range of consecutive numbers or dates. Usually, you can get the same results by creating a formula that increments the previous value and then copying this formula.

To fill a range with consecutive dates, enter a date formula when 1-2-3 asks you for the start value. For example, to get 31 dates starting with January 1, 1993, specify a fill range with at least 31 cells. Enter **@DATE(93,1,1)**. Then, enter **1** for the step value, and **@DATE(93,1,31)** for the stop value. 1-2-3 enters date serial numbers in the fill range, so you have to use the /**R**ange **F**ormat command to make them look like real dates.

/Data Matrix

Inverts square matrices or multiplies matrices. Unless you're an engineer or mathematician, you probably have no use for matrix manipulation. If you're familiar with matrix algebra, you know why you would use this.

Choose one of the following commands and enter the data 1-2-3 asks you for:

Invert	Inverts a matrix.
Multiply	Multiplies a matrix.

More stuff

Actually, there's a use for the **/D**ata **M**atrix **M**ultiply command that even nonmathematicians can appreciate. Let's say that you have a price list stored in a range and you need to increase all prices by 5 percent. You can create formulas to calculate new values and then copy the new values to the old price range. But the **/D**ata **M**atrix **M**ultiply command gives you an easier way: Put the multiplier in an out-of-the-way cell. If you want to increase prices by 5 percent, the multiplier is 1.05 (or 105 percent of the original prices). Choose **/D**ata **M**atrix **M**ultiply. When 1-2-3 asks for the first matrix, highlight the price list. When it asks for the second range, highlight the single multiplier cell. When it asks for an output range, choose a cell to hold the new values. Voila!

/Data Parse

Breaks up a label (usually a long label) into its component parts (or fields) and puts them in separate columns. When you import a text file into 1-2-3, it usually comes in as a bunch of long labels in a single column. Although the file may look good, you find that you cannot do much with it until you break it up (or parse it) into its parts and put each part into a separate column.

Choose the following commands and enter the data 1-2-3 asks you for:

Format-Line	Tells 1-2-3 how to parse the labels. First, choose **C**reate to have 1-2-3 insert a line of codes (see "More stuff"). If you need to change it, choose the **E**dit command.
Input-Column	Specifies the labels that you want to parse as a range.
Output-Range	Specifies the parsed information as a range. You need to specify only a single cell.
Reset	Clears everything you have done with this command. This command is useful if you have blown it and want to start over.
Go	Starts the parsing, using the information you provided.
Quit	Gets out of this menu.

More stuff

The format line that 1-2-3 uses to determine how to parse the labels is fairly cryptic. Basically, this line corresponds to each character in the labels. Here's what the codes mean:

Code	What It Does
D	Begins a date field
L	Begins a label field
S	Skips a block
T	Begins a time field
V	Begins a value field
>	Fills in with whatever code was to the left
*	Enters a blank space

If the labels that you're parsing are consistent, this command works well. But if they aren't consistent, you may be better off reentering the data (or delegating the task) rather than wasting time trying to get it all parsed correctly.

/File Import Text

/Data Query

Searches through a 1-2-3 database to find something that you're looking for. If you have a database set up in a worksheet, using this command is the smart way to find, extract, or delete information that meets your criteria. It takes a bit of upfront work, but the effort pays off.

Choose the following commands and enter the data 1-2-3 asks you for:

Input	Specifies the records to be searched. It can be the complete database or just a part of it.
Criteria	Specifies the criteria (see "More stuff").
Output	Specifies the output (if any). Specifying only one cell is good enough.
Find	Starts the process of finding the records that meet the criteria specified in the Criteria range. In this case, 1-2-3 goes through the data and highlights the rows that qualify. This command is good for browsing.
Extract	Starts the process of extracting records that meet the criteria specified in the Criteria range. 1-2-3 copies these records and sticks them in the Output range you specified.
Unique	Does the same thing as Extract, except that it ignores duplicate records when it copies to the Output range.
Delete	Starts the process of deleting records that meet the criteria specified in the Criteria range.
Reset	Clears the Input, Output, and Criteria ranges. Use this command if you want to start over or use another database.
Quit	Gets out of this menu.

More stuff

To use this command, you must set up a range in your worksheet as a database. You must have column headings that correspond to fields such as FirstName, LastName, City, State, ZIP, and Phone.

You also need a Criteria range that specifies what data you're interested in. The Criteria range is separate from the Database range, but it consists of the same column headings used in the database — plus at least one line of other things. For example, if you want to locate all records that have *Montana* in the State field, you enter **Montana** in the cell directly below the State heading in the Criteria range. To find records that have *Montana* or *Wyoming,* enter these two words in the two cells below the State heading in the Criteria range.

When you set up your Criteria range, make sure that it includes all the rows you use; otherwise, it may miss something. Also, 1-2-3 overwrites the cells in the Output range if they already have something in them (and does not tell you about it). And be sure that the field names in the Criteria range match the Input range exactly.

You can find more information on this command in Chapter 8 of *1-2-3 For Dummies.*

/Data Regression

Performs a statistical analysis to identify linear trends in your data and provides information that lets you predict other values based on existing values. Data regression is pretty cool stuff if you know what you're doing. Most people won't touch this command with a 10-foot pole.

Choose the following commands and enter the data 1-2-3 asks you for:

X-Range	Specifies the independent (or predictor) variables — what's used to predict the dependent variables.
Y-Range	Specifies the dependent variables — what you're interested in predicting.
Output-Range	Specifies the rather cryptic output of this command in the worksheet.
Intercept	Determines whether 1-2-3 computes the y-intercept or forces it to be zero. When in doubt, choose the **C**ompute option.
Reset	Clears everything that you have specified in this command.

Go	Does the regression and puts the results in the Output range.
Quit	Gets out of this menu.

More stuff

Here's an example. The X range holds the heights of 20 people in your office. The Y range holds their weights. A new person is starting work on Monday; you know he's 61 inches tall, and you want to predict his weight. Use the **/D**ata **R**egression command to find out what he will probably weigh. Use the information from the Output-range as follows: multiply the X coefficient by 61 and then add the constant. The result is the predicted weight.

 Usually, you can gain more predictive power if you use more than one predictor variable. For example, you may want to use sex (0 = male, 1 = female) as another predictor variable. This additional predictor would probably make the prediction more accurate. In this case, there would be two X coefficients. Multiply the first by the height, multiply the second by the sex, and then add these to the constant.

 The X range can have more than one column of predictor variables, but the number of data points for each predictor variable must be the same as the number of data points in the Y range. Also, notice that if you change any of your data, you need to repeat the **/D**ata **R**egression command to update the output.

/Data Sort

Sorts a range of data using the column or columns that you specify. The sort can be either ascending or descending. Practically every 1-2-3 user needs to sort data at one time or another. This command lets you see how things look in terms of rankings and also makes finding things easier if they are in some sort of order.

Choose the following commands and enter the data 1-2-3 prompts you for:

Data-Range	Specifies the range to sort.
Primary-Key	Identifies the column that you want to sort by. You need to specify only a single cell in the column.

Secondary-Key	Handles ties (matching data) in the Primary-Key sort. This command is optional.
Reset	Clears the previous three options.
Go	Starts the sorting.
Quit	Gets you out of this menu if you change your mind about sorting.

More stuff

If you're sorting a database, don't include the headings at the top of the columns in the Data range. If you do, they will probably end up somewhere else after the sorting takes place.

When you're sorting a range that's used as a database, make sure that you choose *all* the columns of data. Otherwise, the records may get completely messed up and ruin your whole day. I have seen this happen to many unsuspecting souls who call me up and ask me how their databases got so messed up.

You can find more information on this command in Chapter 8 of *1-2-3 For Dummies*.

/Data Table

Creates a table that shows the effects of using different values of a variable in formulas. Advanced users who want to impress someone use this command.

Choose the following commands and enter the data 1-2-3 prompts you for:

1	Choose this option if you have one input cell that you're varying and one or more dependent formulas.
2	Choose this option if you have two input cells and only one dependent formula.
Reset	Resets everything you have entered for this command.

More stuff

Suppose that you have a worksheet all set up with formulas that depend on a particular cell. The value in this cell may be the purchase price of a house, an interest rate, the unemployment rate, or the number of employees. Chances are that one of these formulas produces a "bottom line" sort of answer. If you change the input cell, you can see what effect it has on the bottom line. Well, the /Data Table command produces a table that shows the results of one or more formulas for a bunch of different values for the input cell. Some people find this very handy.

The key to using this command is to have things set up properly first. You must create a rectangular table. For the first option, put the different input values in the left column of the table and put the formulas that you want to look at in the top row of the rectangle. These formulas can be simple references to other formulas in the worksheet. The upper left corner of the rectangle should be blank. When you issue the /Data Table 1 command, 1-2-3 fills in your rectangular table with the results of the formulas for each value of the input variables.

The /Data Table 2 command lets you look at the results of varying two variables, but you can see only the result on one formula. Put the values for the first variable in the left column of a rectangular range and the values for the second variable in the top row of the rectangle. Put the formula (or a reference to it) in the upper left cell of the rectangle. Issue the command and point out the data. 1-2-3 then asks you for the two input cells. Point to them, and the table fills in.

/File Commands

You may not be surprised to discover that the commands under this menu deal with files. In fact, if you're doing anything that involves a file, the /File command is a good place to start your investigative work.

/File Admin

Gets or releases file reservations and updates links. If you're working on a network, this command can get or release the file reservation so someone else can use the file. If you have file links in your worksheet, this is the place to update them.

Choose the following commands and enter the data 1-2-3 prompts you for:

Reservation   **G**ets or **R**eleases a file reservation.

Table   Inserts an informative table of file information into your worksheet. This command has five options: **W**orksheet, **P**rint, **G**raph, **O**ther, and **L**inked. Be careful, the table may overwrite other stuff in your worksheet.

Link-Refresh   Recalculates formulas that depend on data in other files (links). This reckoning is not done automatically, so if there's a chance that the data in a linked file have changed, you need to issue this command in order to trust your calculations once again.

/File Combine

Copies data from a worksheet on disk to your current worksheet. Besides copying data, you can also add the data to or subtract it from corresponding cells on your current worksheet. This command is often used to consolidate information. If you have a bunch of department budgets in separate worksheets, the /File Combine **A**dd command can roll them up into a grand total.

Choose the following commands and enter the data 1-2-3 prompts you for:

Copy

Replaces information in the current worksheet with the information in the disk file you specify. This command doesn't bring in formulas, just their results. You can use this command to combine several small files into one large file.

Add

Adds the values from the disk file you specify to the corresponding values in the current worksheet.

Subtract

Subtracts the values from the disk file you specify to the corresponding values in the current worksheet.

More stuff

Each of these options has two more options. You need to specify either the **E**ntire File or just a **N**amed/Specified-Range. Cells in your current worksheet that have formulas are not affected by these commands.

If you ever need to "zero out" all the values in a worksheet, you can do it with this trick. Save the worksheet first; then use the /**F**ile Combine **S**ubtract command with the **E**ntire File option. Using this command effectively subtracts each value from itself, which usually works out to be a big zero.

Make sure that you have the cell pointer in the right spot when you issue these commands, because 1-2-3 uses the cell pointer as the upper left cell in the range that it copies, adds, or subtracts.

Because 1-2-3 doesn't do any type of checking to make sure what you're trying to do is logical, you have to be on your toes. If you're consolidating a group of budget worksheets, for example, each worksheet must be laid out identically. Otherwise, you can end up doing something embarrassing, like adding salaries to photocopying expenses.

/File Directory

Changes the current "working" directory that 1-2-3 uses to save and retrieve files from. If you're working on a bunch of files that are not in your default directory, using this command makes retrieving them easier, because you don't have to change the directory manually every time you issue the /File Retrieve command.

More stuff

This command affects only the current session; it doesn't change the default directory permanently.

/Worksheet Global Default Directory

/File Erase

Zaps a file off your disk. This command is basically a convenience that keeps you from having to use the DOS DEL command to erase a file. If your disk has suddenly filled up to the extent that you can't even save your current worksheet, this command lets you free up some space by getting rid of one or more files that you no longer need.

Choose the following commands and enter the data 1-2-3 prompts you for:

Worksheet	Lists all worksheet files (*.WK?) in the current directory.
Print	Lists all print files (*.PRN) in the current directory.
Graph	Lists all graph files (*.PIC) in the current directory.
Other	Lists all files (*.*) in the current directory.

More stuff

If the file you want to nuke isn't in the current directory, press Backspace to "move up" in the directory tree and choose the directory you're interested in.

Don't confuse this command with the /**R**ange **E**rase command, which erases a part of your current worksheet.

The results of this command are permanent. You can't go back after a file has been erased from your disk — unless, of course, you have a pal who knows how to "unerase" files. If you ever discover that you accidentally deleted a good file, don't save anything else to the disk. Ways to bring a deleted file back from the dead are available — and you stand a much better chance of doing so if you don't save anything after your mess up.

Also, be careful with the **O**ther option because this command makes erasing important files that are necessary to run 1-2-3 very easy.

/File Import

Brings in an ASCII (or text) file from disk. You probably know that there are lots of different types of files, and software cannot always read files created by other software. Most programs, however, can save their data as a plain ASCII file. Because most programs can read ASCII files, they serve as sort of the lowest common denominator among programs.

Choose the following commands and enter the data that 1-2-3 asks you for:

Text   Sticks each line of the text file into a single cell and treats it as a label. You often need to use the /**D**ata **P**arse command to break these labels.

Numbers   Examines the text file for characters that look like numbers and brings in only the numbers. For each line of the text file, each number is put in a separate column in your worksheet. For some files this works well; for others you need to do some manual clean-up work.

More stuff

After you choose the **T**ext or **N**umbers option, 1-2-3 displays a list of files with a PRN extension. If the file you want to bring in has a different extension, you need to add your own specification. For example, if you enter ***.***, 1-2-3 shows you all the files in the directory.

Text files are very generic and never have specific formatting information, such as bold, underlining, and margins. Because they are nonexclusive, they are interchangeable between computer programs.

/**D**ata **P**arse

/File List

Shows you a list of files of a particular type. This command isn't all that useful, unless you really want to know where a particular file is or something like when it was saved or how big it is. If you're looking for a file to load in, the /**F**ile **R**etrieve command does the same thing — and also lets you load the file in the same command.

Choose the following commands and enter the data that 1-2-3 asks you for:

Worksheet Lists all worksheet files (*.WK?) in the current directory.

Print Lists all print files (*.PRN) in the current directory.

Graph Lists all graph files (*.PIC) in the current directory.

Other Lists all files (*.*) in the current directory.

Linked Lists all files to which the current worksheet is linked.

/**F**ile **A**dmin **T**able

/File Retrieve

Loads a worksheet file from the disk into 1-2-3. This command is the most popular way to load existing information into 1-2-3. You won't get too far in 1-2-3 without using this command.

More stuff

1-2-3 lists all the worksheet files in the current directory. If the file you want to retrieve is somewhere else, you can press Backspace to traverse the directories or enter the complete file spec (drive, path, and filename) manually.

If you use only one worksheet, you can save yourself a few seconds by loading the worksheet along with 1-2-3. Let's say you want to load DAILY.WK1 every time you start 1-2-3. Use this command from the DOS prompt to start 1-2-3: **1-2-3 -wDAILY** (the **-w** is followed immediately (no space) by the filename, which must be in the default directory).

Because 1-2-3 can deal with only one worksheet at a time, the **/F**ile **R**etrieve command dumps the current worksheet and replaces it with the one you want. But this is really no cause for concern. 1-2-3 always lets you know this exchange is about to happen and gives you the chance to back out. It also warns you if your current worksheet has not been saved.

You can find more information on this command in Chapter 4 of *1-2-3 For Dummies.*

/File Save

Saves the current worksheet to a file on disk. This command can best be described as essential (unless, of course, you don't want to save what you have done). If you don't save your work to a file, it will be gone the next time you turn on your computer. In other words, this command gives your hard drive something to do.

Choose the following commands, which appear only if the worksheet already has a name or you choose the name of an existing file, and enter the data that 1-2-3 asks you for:

Cancel   Gets you out of this command. Use this command if you get cold feet and decide not to save the worksheet after all.

Replace   Replaces the existing disk file with a new file that contains your worksheet stuff. More often than not, you will want to use this command.

Backup   Renames the existing disk file with a BAK extension and saves the worksheet with the normal WK1 extension. This command is useful if you don't want to destroy the version of your worksheet that existed before you made changes to it.

More stuff

The first time you save a file, 1-2-3 asks you for a filename. You can use up to eight characters (no spaces). 1-2-3 provides the WK1 extension for the file. If the worksheet already has a name, 1-2-3 prompts you with the existing filename, and you just press Enter to save it.

If you're using the Wysiwyg add-in, 1-2-3 also saves an additional file with the same filename, but with an FMT extension. This is the formatting information that goes with the worksheet.

If you're working on something that you don't want anybody else to see, you can save the file with a password. If you do so, the snoop who tries to load the file with the /File **R**etrieve command must type the password before 1-2-3 loads it. The procedure for saving a file with a password is not really obvious, but here's how to do it. When you type in the filename, don't press Enter. Rather, add a space, type **P**, and then press Enter. 1-2-3 then lets you type in the password — and it makes you do it twice for your own protection.

As thousands of people have probably told you by now, save your work often. This is especially true if the electrical power in your building isn't too stable. Also, if you look out the window and see lightning, take this as a signal to save your work frequently. Whenever the power goes off in my office, I can always tell who's using their PC because their voices are part of a collective obscenity.

If you save a file with a password, don't forget the password because there's no way to load a password-protected file without it (even 1-2-3 gurus cannot rescue you from this one). Also, passwords entered must be exact — including case. This means that typing **GOOP** when the password is **goop** won't let you load it.

You can find more information on this command in Chapter 1 of *1-2-3 For Dummies*.

/File Xtract

Saves only a portion of the current worksheet to a file. This command is useful if you want to break up a worksheet into different parts or if you want to give somebody only part of a worksheet that's relevant to them.

Choose the following commands and enter the data that 1-2-3 asks you for:

Formulas — Saves the data and the formulas in the range you specify.

Values — Saves only the current values in the range you specify (no formulas).

More stuff

When you issue this command, you go through three steps. First, 1-2-3 asks you whether you want to save the range as **F**ormulas or **V**alues. It then asks for a filename (you can use an existing file or enter a new filename). Finally, it asks you to choose the range that you want to extract.

Settings from the current worksheet (print settings, range names, and so on) are saved with the file you extract to.

You can use the /**F**ile **C**ombine command to bring the extracted information back into the worksheet. This lets you set up different scenarios.

If you use the **F**ormulas option, make sure that the range you extract also includes the cells that the formulas refer to (if any). Otherwise, you are in for a rude awakening when you find that the formulas in the extracted file don't produce the right results.

Also, make sure that your worksheet is calculated before extracting anything from it. If CALC shows up at the bottom of the screen, press the F9 key before doing the /**F**ile **X**tract.

/**P**rint **F**ile
/**F**ile **C**ombine

You can find more information on this command in Chapter 8 of *1-2-3 For Dummies.*

/Graph Commands

Surveys show that nine out of ten 1-2-3 users who want to make a graph start out with the /Graph command. This command displays a dialog box that makes specifying your graph parameters relatively easy. If you use this dialog box, you may not even have to use the seemingly endless series of commands under the /Graph command.

/Graph A, B, C, D, E, F

Defines the range or ranges of data that are graphed. If you're making a graph, it needs to have at least one data range.

More stuff

A graph can have up to six data ranges, labeled A through F. When 1-2-3 asks you to enter the data range, you can highlight it or enter a range name.

If you are graphing only one data range, you usually use the /Graph **A** command to specify it. But actually, you can use any of the six letters. The graph letter that you use determines the color that is graphed.

/Graph **Group**
/Graph **X**

You can find more information on this command in Chapter 7 of *1-2-3 For Dummies.*

/Graph Group

Lets you specify all graph ranges in one fell swoop. If your data to be graphed are all together in one range, this command saves you the trouble of specifying each range separately.

First specify the group range.

Choose the following commands and enter the data that 1-2-3 asks you for:

Columnwise   Interprets the group range vertically (each graph range is in a separate column).

Rowwise   Interprets the group range horizontally (each graph range is in a separate row).

More stuff

If you choose **C**olumnwise, the first column of the group range holds the X range, and each successive column holds range A, B, and so on. If you choose **R**owwise, the first row of the group range holds the X range, and each row under it holds range A, B, and so on.

When you tell 1-2-3 what the group range is, don't include labels that you eventually need to use for the legend. If you do use these labels, 1-2-3 interprets them as zero values, and your graph won't be right. Unfortunately, 1-2-3 isn't smart enough to set up legends for you.

/Graph **A, B, C, D, E, F**
/Graph **X**

You can find more information on this command in Chapter 7 of *1-2-3 For Dummies.*

/Graph Name

Lets you work with graphs using their names. You need to use this command only if your worksheet has more than one graph. If you have several graphs, each one has to have a name because 1-2-3 can deal with only one graph at a time (the "current graph"). A graph name is actually just a name for all the settings that a graph has (X range, data ranges, titles, and so on).

Choose the following commands and enter the data that 1-2-3 asks you for:

Use   Switches to a different named graph and displays it.

Create   Lets you give a name for the current graph.

Delete   Deletes an unneeded graph name.

Reset   Removes all graph names and their settings in the current worksheet.

Table   Sticks a table in the worksheet that shows all the named graphs, their graph type, and their first title.

More stuff

Using names that are meaningful and describe what the graph shows is a good idea.

Be careful with the /**G**raph **N**ame **R**eset command because you can lose a lot of graph work if you get a little a careless. 1-2-3 doesn't provide a warning that it's about to destroy all graph names and settings.

If you make any changes to a graph that has a name, you need to remember to use the /**G**raph **N**ame **C**reate command to save the changed graph settings (this is not done automatically, as you may expect). Usually, you specify the same name that it had — unless you want to have names for both the original and the changed version.

You can find more information on this command in Chapter 7 of *1-2-3 For Dummies.*

/Graph Options

Lets you customize graphs in several ways. If you're not satisfied with the default look that 1-2-3 gives a newly created graph (which is usually the case), you can change it and add things to it.

Choose the following commands and enter the data that 1-2-3 asks you for:

Legend
: Lets you enter legend text for each graph range. You can also enter a reference to a worksheet cell by preceding the cell reference with a backslash. For example, entering **\A12** uses the contents of cell A12 for the legend text.

Format
: Lets you specify how the graphed data for a range appears. You can specify **L**ines, **S**ymbols, **B**oth, **N**either, or **A**rea, and you can have different formats for each range. This command is relevant only for line, XY, or mixed graphs.

Titles
: Lets you enter text for various title areas in a graph. The four title areas are **F**irst, **S**econd, **X**-Axis, and **Y**-Axis. You can enter a reference to a worksheet cell by preceding the cell reference with a backslash. For example, entering **\B4** uses the contents of cell B4 for the title.

Grid
: Lets you specify the type of background grid (if any) you want. Your choices are: **H**orizontal, **V**ertical, or **B**oth. Choosing **C**lear gets rid of any grid on the graph.

Scale
: Lets you specify various aspects of the scaling for the x-axis and y-axis. The **S**kip option lets you skip some entries on the x-axis (useful if the words are all crammed together). This option leads to a lot more options. For example, you can specify the **U**pper and **L**ower limits for the x- and y-axes rather than letting 1-2-3 figure it out. You can also turn the **S**cale Indicator on or off. The scale indicator is something like "(Thousands)" or "(Millions)" that tell you the order of magnitude of the data graphed.

Color
: Shows the graph in color.

B&W
: Shows the graph in boring black and white.

Data Labels
: Lets you tell 1-2-3 what labels to display on the graph for each data range.

Quit
: Gets you out of the /Graph Options menu.

More stuff

Tons of options are lurking below the **/Graph O**ptions command, and the menus sometimes seem to go on forever. I can easily go on for four or five more pages, but that discussion would make for boring reading. Take my advice and use the dialog boxes that pop up when you issue the **/G**raph command. This dialog box shows all the settings and lets you change them without fear of getting lost in the menus.

You can find more information on this command in Chapter 7 of *1-2-3 For Dummies.*

/Graph Quit

Gets you out of the **/G**raph menu and returns you to the comfort and familiar surroundings of your worksheet.

/Graph Reset

Restores some or all the current graph's settings to the default. If you find that you have totally messed up a graph by trying to customize it with various options, this command lets you start over.

Choose the following commands and enter the data that 1-2-3 asks you for:

Graph	Clears all the graph settings.
X	Clears the settings only for the X range.
A, B, C, D, E, F	Removes the data range you specify from the graph.
Ranges	Clears all the data range plus the X range.
Options	Clears one of the options settings.
Quit	Gets you back to the **/G**raph menu.

Be careful that you don't clear an entire graph range when you wanted to clear out only the settings for the range.

/Graph Save

Saves the current graph picture in a separate file. This command lets you print the graph using the PrintGraph program or saves the graph in a format that you can use with the Wysiwyg add-in. If you happen to have some other software that can read Lotus' PIC graph format files, you can save a graph with this command and then import the file into your other software.

More stuff

You have to enter a filename for this command. 1-2-3 adds the PIC extension. If the filename already exists, 1-2-3 tells you so.

/Graph Type

Chooses the format (line, bar, area, and so on) for the current graph. If you're not happy with the default line graph 1-2-3 generates, change it here.

Choose the following commands and enter the data that 1-2-3 asks you for:

Line	Turns the current graph into a line graph.
Bar	Turns the current graph into a bar graph.
X-Y	Turns the current graph into an XY graph. You have to have an X range defined for this to work; otherwise, the graph is an empty screen.
Stack-Bar	Turns the current graph into a stacked bar graph.
Pie	Turns the current graph into a pie graph. You have to have an A range defined for this to work; otherwise, the graph is an empty screen.

HLCO	Turns the current graph into a stock market graph showing high, low, closing, and opening prices. You need to have the A range (high values), B range (low value), C range (close values), and D range (open values) defined.
Mixed	Turns the current graph into a combination bar - line graph. The A, B, and C ranges turn into bars, and the D, E, and F ranges show up as lines. You may need to reassign the ranges to get this to work as you want.
Features	Lets you change some other aspects of the graph. This leads you down another long menu path, so it's best to use the dialog box that's displayed.

In general, you cannot simply change the graph type haphazardly and expect the modification to work. Not all data can be graphed appropriately using all the different graph types.

You can find more information on this command in Chapter 7 of *1-2-3 For Dummies.*

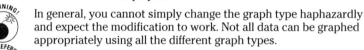

/Graph View

Displays the current graph in full-screen mode. If you want to see what a graph looks like, this command does it.

More stuff

You can also press the F10 key at just about any point to accomplish the same end.

/Graph X

Defines the range of data that will serve as the X-Axis labels, or X Range in an XY graph.

Some graphs need an x-axis range. The X range is also used for labels that appear at the bottom of the graph. The months of the year are good example.

More stuff

For line and bar graphs, the X range usually consists of labels that show up at the bottom of the graph. For a pie graph, the X range provides labels for the pie slices. For an XY graph, the X range provides values that are plotted against the Y values.

 /**Graph G**roup

/Move Command

Moves a cell or range from one location to another. Moving data around in a worksheet is a very common operation when you're creating a worksheet. The fact is, hardly anybody gets it right the first time.

More stuff

When you issue this command, 1-2-3 asks you, Move what? Respond by highlighting the range to be moved and pressing Enter. It then asks you, To where? Move the cell pointer to the new location and press Enter. If you're moving a range, you need to specify only the upper left cell.

As you may expect, this command also moves formats along with the cell contents. If you have the Wysiwyg add-in loaded, the Wysiwyg formats come along for the ride.

The /**M**ove command automatically adjusts formulas that are moved and also causes formulas that refer to the moved cells to adjust themselves. This is what you would expect; otherwise, moving cells and ranges would mess up everything.

 Like the /**C**opy command, this one can cause problems if you're not careful. 1-2-3 won't warn you if you move a range to an area that already contains information. The current data are wiped out by the stuff that you moved. They are gone to that big byte bucket in the sky.

 You can find more information on this command in Chapter 4 of *1-2-3 For Dummies*.

/Print Commands

When it's time to get your masterpiece on paper, **/P** is the name of the game. This command also does some other things, like send output to a file instead of the printer.

/Print Background

Sends a range to an encoded file and then prints it in the background while you continue on your merry way. If you have a lot of printing to do, this command lets you continue working while the printing is being done. On the other hand, waiting for your work to print is a good excuse for taking a break.

More stuff

This command works by creating a file on disk that holds the stuff to be printed. Therefore, 1-2-3 asks you for a filename to hold the printed output before it's sent to the printer. It automatically adds the ENC extension. But you're not done yet; you still have to go through the normal /Print **P**rinter business in order to tell 1-2-3 what you want printed.

 In order to do background printing, you must have run the BPRINT program before you started 1-2-3. Don't try to use the /System command to exit to DOS temporarily and run BPRINT — it won't work.

/Print Encoded

Creates a special encoded file that contains everything that would normally be sent to a printer (including all the cryptic printer-specific codes that only a computer wiz can understand).

This command can be pretty handy if you don't have a printer hooked up (a common occurrence for laptop users on an airplane). Instead of printing to a printer, you print to a file. Then, when you get back on the ground, you can copy this file to the printer, and it looks just like it would have looked if you had the printer on the plane with you. The DOS command to copy a file to a printer is

COPY filename.ENC PRN

Choose the following commands and enter the data that 1-2-3 asks you for:

Range	Lets you identify the range that you want to send to the file.
Line	Sends a blank line to the file.
Page	Sends a page break to the file.
Options	Lets you set a bunch of options (**H**eader, **F**ooter, **M**argins, **B**orders, **S**etup, **P**g-Length, and **O**ther). Rather than use the menus, it's easier to take advantage of the dialog box that 1-2-3 displays.
Clear	Lets you clear all the settings or just selected ones.
Align	Resets the top of page on the "printer," which is really an encoded file, remember.
Go	Makes the encoded file.
Quit	Gets you out of this menu.

More stuff

1-2-3 asks you for a filename to hold the printed output before it's sent to the printer. It automatically adds the ENC extension.

The encoded file that's produced is custom-made for the printer that you have installed in 1-2-3. If you try to copy this file to a different printer, the results may be complete gibberish. And don't even think about loading an encoded file back into 1-2-3 because the program won't know what to do with it.

/Print File

Sends a specified worksheet range to an ASCII file. If you need to use some 1-2-3 worksheet data in a program that cannot read 1-2-3 files, this command lets you save work in a plain old garden variety text (ASCII) file, which most applications can read.

Choose the following commands and enter the data that 1-2-3 asks you for:

Range	Lets you indicate the range that you want to send to the file.
Line	Sends a blank line to the file.
Page	Makes the file skip to the top of the next page.
Options	Lets you set options (**H**eader, **F**ooter, **M**argins, **B**orders, **S**etup, **P**g-Length, and **O**ther). Most of the time, you want to choose the **O**ther Unformatted option when you print to a text file.
Clear	Lets you clear all the settings or just selected ones.
Align	Resets the top of page on text file.
Go	Starts writing to the file.
Quit	Gets you out of this menu.

More stuff

1-2-3 saves this with a PRN extension. If you don't like this, override it by typing another extension such as TXT.

/**F**ile Extract

/Print Printer

Sends a specified worksheet range to the printer. This is how to print stuff from 1-2-3.

Choose the following commands and enter the data that 1-2-3 asks you for:

Range	Lets you indicate the range that you want to print.
Line	Sends a blank line to the printer.
Page	Sets the printer up to start at the top of a new page.
Options	Lets you set options (**H**eader, **F**ooter, **M**argins, **B**orders, **S**etup, **P**g-Length, and **O**ther). Rather than use the menus, it's easier to take advantage of the dialog box that 1-2-3 displays.

Clear	Lets you clear all the settings or just selected ones.
Align	Resets the top of page on the printer.
Go	Lets the printing begin.
Quit	Gets you out of this menu.

More stuff

You can also use the Wysiwyg **:P**rint menu if you want to print fancy stuff.

If you use the Wysiwyg add-in, be aware that the printing options you set using the **/P**rint menu have nothing to do with the printing options you set on the Wysiwyg **:P**rint menu. For example, if you set the print range with the **/P**rint **R**ange command, the Wysiwyg **:P**rint command won't know about it. These two menus systems seem to be feuding and refuse to speak to each other.

:Print

You can find more information on this command in Chapter 6 of *1-2-3 For Dummies*.

/Quit Command

Ready to call it a day? This command shuts down 1-2-3 so you can say your good-byes and close up shop. When you're finished using a computer program, it's a good practice to go through the normal exit procedures rather than just turn off the machine. This also makes 1-2-3 check to make sure that you don't have any unsaved data. If you just want to exit temporarily to do something like rename a file, you can use the **/S**ystem command.

/System

You can find more information on this command in Chapter 1 of *1-2-3 For Dummies*.

/Range Commands

This group of commands manipulates — you guessed it — ranges.

/Range Erase

Erases the contents of a cell or range. Using this command is the fastest way to clear out the contents of a range.

More stuff

After you choose this command, 1-2-3 prompts you for the range to erase. If it's a single cell, just press Enter. Otherwise, point out the range to be zapped and then press Enter.

 To erase a single cell, it's easier just to press Delete.

This command does not wipe out cell formats. Use the /Range Format Reset command to get rid of any unwanted formats in a cell or range.

 When you erase a range, it's gone for good. So make sure this is really what you want to do.

I have seen many 1-2-3 users clear out a cell by pressing the spacebar. Actually, this practice can cause problems later on. Putting a space into a cell is not the same as erasing it. Although the cell may appear to be blank, it is not empty. So if somebody tells you about this fast way to erase a single cell, tell them about Delete.

/Range Format

Determines how numbers look on your worksheet and when printed. Normally, when you enter a value into a cell, 1-2-3 uses its General format. Whenever you want your numbers to look different — change the number of decimal places, use commas, add a percent sign, and so on — here's where you do it.

Choose the following commands and enter the data that 1-2-3 asks you for:

Fixed

Displays numbers in the range with a fixed number of decimal places (2 is the default, but you can enter any number between **0** and **15**).

Sci

Displays numbers in the range in exponential form, which is the power of 10 that the number must be multiplied by. For example, the scientific format for one hundred million (100,000,000) is 1.0E+08. This means *1 times 10 to the eighth power.*

Currency

Displays numbers in the range in currency form. This means the numbers have a dollar sign before them, they have comma separators, and negative numbers are in parentheses.

,

Displays numbers in the range in comma format. The numbers displayed by this command look the same as those displayed by the Currency command, but without the dollar signs.

General

Displays numbers in the range in 1-2-3's default format. Trailing zeros don't show, and very large or small numbers show up in scientific format.

+/−

Displays numbers in the range as a bunch of plus or minus signs. This command is actually used to produce crude horizontal bar graphs that show the relative size of numbers.

Percent

Displays numbers in the range in percentage format. In effect, each entry is multiplied by 100 and a % sign is tacked on to the end.

Date

Displays numbers in the range as one of five date formats. This leads to another menu where you choose the date. This secondary menu has an option called Time, which leads to several different time formats you can choose from. Formatting a range as Date or Time makes sense only when the numbers are 1-2-3 date serial numbers.

Text

Displays everything in the range exactly as you entered it — including formulas. This can be useful if you want to see the formulas, not their results.

Hidden	Makes everything in the range invisible. However, if you move the cell pointer to such a hidden cell, you can see its contents in the control panel at the top of the screen.
Reset	Resets the range to 1-2-3's current global format (which you can change using the /Worksheet Global Format command).

More stuff

It's important to understand that the /Format command affects only how numbers appear. It does not change the actual values at all. For example, if you format 12.3469 for two decimal places, it appears as 12.35. However, 1-2-3 continues to use the actual 12.3469 value.

If the column is not wide enough to accommodate the format you specified, 1-2-3 displays a bunch of asterisks (**********). To get the numbers to show up, use the /Worksheet Column Set-Width command (or use the SmartIcon that adjusts the column to fit the widest number).

Formats that you apply with the /Format command take precedence over the worksheet's global format. So if you change the global format with the /Worksheet Global command, it affects only the cells that have not been formatted with /Format.

Most of the format options already described also let you specify the number of decimal places you want to show.

There are several SmartIcons that apply a specific numeric format with a single click of the rodent.

/Worksheet Global Format

You can find more information on this command in Chapter 3 of *1-2-3 For Dummies.*

/Range Input

Limits the cell pointer to move only to unprotected cells in a range. This command is useful if you have a worksheet set up with some cells designated as input values. Changing one or more of the input values causes the whole thing to recalculate and show new results. If you protect all cells except the input values, the /**R**ange **I**nput command does not let anyone move the cell pointer to any noninput cells. It's also handy for worksheets set up as fill-in-the-blanks forms.

More stuff

Before you use this command, use /**R**ange **U**nprot to designate the input cells (the cells that are OK to move the cell pointer to). After you issue the /**R**ange **I**nput command and point out the range, the cell pointer moves to the input cells only.

You get out of this mode simply by pressing Enter or Esc.

/**R**ange **U**nprot

/Range Justify

Rearranges text in a range by wrapping words according to the width you specify. If you have a bunch of labels in a worksheet that you use for instructions or explanatory stuff, this command lets you easily change the text and then reformat the whole shebang so it looks good and aligned.

More stuff

Assume you have some instructions in a worksheet in the form of labels. These labels are in the range A1..A10, and they spill over about four columns to the right. You want to add a few more words to the label in cell A4, but doing so makes the label stick out like a sore thumb because it's much longer than the others. Choose /**R**ange **J**ustify. Highlight the range A1..E10 (assuming you want the labels to spill over no further than column E). Press Enter and 1-2-3 reformats all the labels and wrap the words around to make them all the same width.

This command takes some getting used to, but it's worth learning if you tend to use a lot of text in your worksheets.

If the reformatted text won't fit in the range you specify, 1-2-3 does as much as it can and then lets you know the rest won't fit. Choose all the labels, specify a wider range, and try again.

/Range Label

Lets you choose how labels are aligned (left, right, or centered). When you enter a label, you can precede it with a label prefix: a single quote (') for left aligned, a double quote (") for right aligned, or a caret (^) for centered. This command changes the label prefixes for one cell or a range of cells. If you have a bunch of labels you need to change, it's much faster than editing each one manually.

Choose the following commands and enter the data that 1-2-3 asks you for:

Left	Aligns the labels on the left.
Right	Aligns the labels on the right.
Center	Centers the labels in their cell.

More stuff

Right-aligned labels may not appear to be aligned on the right if the column is not wider than the number of characters in the label. The same goes for centered labels.

Oddly enough, 1-2-3 can't change the alignment of values — they are always right aligned in their cell.

If you use Wysiwyg, this add-in has many more options for dealing with text. For example, you can center a single label over a group of columns.

You can find more information on this command in Chapter 3 of *1-2-3 For Dummies.*

/Range Name

Gives a name to a cell or a range. Naming cells and ranges is an excellent habit to get into. If you give range B1..B20 a name such as *Expenses,* you can write a formula like this: @SUM(expenses). Using this procedure makes your formulas much easier to read and understand. And people who look at your spreadsheets will be impressed with your organization. Naming cells and ranges also makes finding stuff easier. You can, for example, press the F5 (Goto) key, and 1-2-3 shows a list of all the named ranges and cells. Choose the one you want, and you're there in a jiff.

Choose the following commands and enter the data that 1-2-3 asks you for:

Create | Assigns a name to a cell or range.

Delete | Deletes the name assigned to a range of cell (it doesn't delete the actual cell or range).

Labels | Creates names for single cells using labels stored on your worksheet. The labels can be to the left, right, above, or below the cells you want to name. After issuing the /**R**ange **N**ame **L**abels command, tell 1-2-3 where the cells to be named are in relation to the labels. Then highlight the labels and the cells you're naming.

Reset | Wipes out all names in a worksheet.

Table | Makes a list of all range names and the range that they refer to and sticks the list in the worksheet for reference.

More stuff

Range names can be up to 15 characters long, and 1-2-3 doesn't care about upper- or lowercase in your range names. However, you cannot use spaces or any of these characters in a range name:

+ * - / & > < @ # { , ;

Avoid creating range names that look like cell references. For example, a range named *A24* is acceptable to 1-2-3, but you shouldn't use it because A24 is also the name of a cell. Using this system of naming ranges can cause major problems that you can't foresee until it's too late.

If you move the cell that makes up the corner of a range that has a name, the range referred to by the name is not what it was originally. Also be careful with the /**R**ange **N**ame **R**eset command. This can quickly wipe out every range name in your worksheet before you know it (and 1-2-3 doesn't give you a warning).

You can find more information on this command in Chapter 9 of *1-2-3 For Dummies.*

/Range Prot

Protects cells in a range. This command keeps others (or yourself) from changing the contents of a cell. Savvy 1-2-3 users often protect their formula cells after they get them working properly so they won't accidentally be erased or overwritten with a value.

More stuff

This command does not have any effect if global protection is not enabled.

/**R**ange **U**prot
/**W**orksheet **G**lobal **P**rotection

/Range Search

Finds a certain text string in labels or formulas and (optionally) replaces it with something else. You use this command when you need to find a string that you know is somewhere in your worksheet but you don't want to sit and press PgDn to try to find it. You can also use the Replace option of this command to make global changes to a worksheet. For example, you can replace every occurrence of `Budget94` with `Budget95`.

After you issue the /**R**ange **S**earch command, 1-2-3 asks you for two things: the range to search and the string to search for. It then gives you three options:

Formulas	Searches for the string in cells that have formulas.
Labels	Searches for the string in cells that have labels.
Both	Searches for the string in cells that have either labels or formulas.

More stuff

After you specify where to search and what to search , grills you for even more information. It wants to know whe, you want to find just the string or replace it with something. It y choose **R**eplace, it asks you what you want to replace it with. Finally, it gives you the option of replacing them all or deciding on a case-by-case basis.

If you enter a number as the string to search for, 1-2-3 looks for the number only if it's in a string or a formula. In other words, you cannot search for actual values.

/Range Trans

Makes a copy of a range, flip flopping it so the rows turn into columns and the columns turn into rows.

More stuff

1-2-3 first asks you for the range to transpose and then asks you where to transpose it. In response to the second question, you can enter just the upper left cell.

This command makes a copy of the range — it doesn't move it.

There's a major hitch in this transposition stuff: All the formulas in the range that you transpose are converted to values. Usually, this is not what you want. Therefore, this command is most useful for ranges that don't have any formulas.

/Range Unprot

Removes the protection status from cells in a range. This command lets you make changes to cells when worksheet global protection is enabled.

/System Command

Lets you issue DOS commands without exiting 1-2-3. In technical terms, this command "shells out" to DOS and keeps 1-2-3 loaded in memory.

More stuff

To get back to 1-2-3 when you're finished using DOS, type **EXIT** at the DOS prompt.

After you use the **/**System command, 1-2-3 disappears from your screen. It's easy to forget that 1-2-3 is still active, and you may be tempted to simply turn off your computer and leave your worries behind. If you do flip off the computer, 1-2-3 won't have a chance to warn you if you haven't saved your work — and you can lose your latest changes.

/Worksheet Commands

This series of commands does things with the worksheet as a whole.

/Worksheet Column

Changes the way a column or group of columns look. You often need to make columns wider so numbers don't appear as asterisks. Also, you can hide columns so others won't see them, or so they won't be printed.

Choose the following commands and enter the data that 1-2-3 asks you for:

Set-Width	Changes the width of the current column to a width you specify. You can either enter a number of characters or use ← and → to adjust the column width while you watch.
Reset-Width	Changes the width of the current column to the global default column width.
Hide	Hides a column range from view. The values and formulas still work; you just can't see them.
Display	Unhides hidden columns. When you choose this option, the invisible columns suddenly become visible so you can choose which ones to unhide.
Column-Range	Lets you change the width of a group of columns at the same time. This has two more options: **S**et-Width and **R**eset-Width.

More stuff

Setting a column width takes precedence over the global column width, which you can change with the **/W**orksheet **G**lobal **C**olumn-Width command. In other words, changing the global column width has no effect on those columns for which you have adjusted the width.

/Worksheet **G**lobal **C**olumn-Width

You can find more information on this command in Chapter 3 of *1-2-3 For Dummies.*

/Worksheet Delete

Removes columns or rows (including their contents). If you want to get rid of everything in a row or column, this command is the fastest way to do so.

Choose the following commands and enter the data that 1-2-3 asks you for:

Column   Deletes one or more columns.

Row   Deletes one or more rows.

More stuff

When you issue this command, 1-2-3 asks you to enter the range of columns or rows to delete. Highlight cells to indicate what you want to do and press Enter. Bye-bye.

/**R**ange **E**rase
/**W**orksheet **I**nsert

You can find more information on this command in Chapter 4 of *1-2-3 For Dummies.*

/Worksheet Erase

Zaps the entire worksheet and leaves you with a million or so empty cells. This command is used when you're ready to start building a new worksheet and want to clear things out. Unless you want to start over completely, you normally need to save your worksheet before issuing this command.

Choose one of the following commands:

No   Lets you change your mind.

Yes   Lets you go for it.

More stuff

1-2-3 warns you if you haven't saved your work. Also, be aware that this command does not affect files stored on disk.

/File Erase

You can find more information on this command in Chapter 4 of *1-2-3 For Dummies.*

Worksheet Global

Lets you specify how 1-2-3 is configured. Use this command to customize some aspects of how 1-2-3 does its thing.

Choose the following commands and enter the data that 1-2-3 asks you for:

Format	Lets you choose the default numeric format (normally, it's **G**eneral).
Label-Prefix	Lets you choose the default label prefix (normally, it's a single quote (') or left-aligned labels).
Column-Width	Lets you choose the default column width (normally, it's nine characters).
Recalculation	Lets you determine how 1-2-3 recalculates its formulas. This leads to another menu with several more options. Normally, you want your formulas to calculate automatically. If you're working on a massive worksheet with zillions of formulas, you may want to set it to **M**anual. If the recalculation is set to manual, you can force a recalculation by pressing F9.

Protection	Lets you specify whether worksheet protection is on or off.
Default	Lets you set other settings: **P**rinter, **D**irectory, **S**tatus, **U**pdate, **O**ther, and **A**utoexec. Here's a case where the menus get pretty deep, so do yourself a favor and use the dialog box instead of the menus.
Zero	Lets you choose how zero values appear. The choices are **N**o (show blanks), **Y**es (show zeros), or **L**abel (display a label that you specify).

More stuff

If you change any of the default settings with the /**W**orksheet **G**lobal **D**efault command, you can make these changes permanent by using the Update option. That way, the defaults are in effect the next time you run 1-2-3.

Settings that you make in this menu do not override those that you make elsewhere. For example, if you change the global column width, it does not affect columns that you previously set a column width for.

You can find more information on this command in Chapter 3 of *1-2-3 For Dummies.*

/Worksheet Insert

Inserts new (blank) columns or rows in a worksheet. If you need to insert something in between two rows (or two columns), this command is much easier than moving the ranges around to make space for the new stuff.

Choose the following commands and enter the data that 1-2-3 asks you for:

Column	Inserts one or more columns to the left of the column that holds the cell pointer.
Row	Inserts one or more rows above the row that holds the cell pointer.

More stuff

As you may expect, all the formulas in your worksheet are adjusted automatically to account for the shifting cells. The new rows or columns are blank and unformatted.

Columns are moved to the right and rows are moved down to accommodate the new stuff. If the last row has something in it, you cannot use the /Worksheet Insert Row command because there's no place for the last row to go. The same thing is true for the /Worksheet Insert Column command if the last column has something in it.

 If you ever want to fix it so someone (or yourself) cannot insert new rows or columns, simply put something (anything) in cell IV8192. Attempting to insert a row or column causes 1-2-3 to tell you that the worksheet is full.

 You can find more information on this command in Chapter 4 of *1-2-3 For Dummies.*

/Worksheet Learn

Captures keystrokes you make in preparation for creating a macro. If you're creating a macro that simply plays back keystrokes, using this command is the easiest way to do it.

Choose the following commands and enter the data that 1-2-3 asks you for:

Range — A single-column range that holds the keystrokes you make.

Cancel — Cancels the learn range that you previously specified (the stuff already there stays there).

Erase — Clears out the keystrokes in a learn range that you specified.

 If the learn range fills up, 1-2-3 issues an error message, and you cannot continue recording until you enlarge the learn range. Normally, you have to erase what you have done and start over.

 You can find more information on this command in Chapter 9 of *1-2-3 For Dummies.*

/Worksheet Page

Inserts a page break code that controls what happens when you print. When you're printing, you often want to control when the page breaks occur. For example, you may want information for each sales office to start printing on a separate page. Inserting a page break code is much easier than trying to insert new rows so the page breaks happen in the right spots.

More stuff

The page break code is :: (two colons). This command puts this code into the current cell and moves all the rows below it down one row to make room for it. Before you issue this command, make sure the cell pointer is in the row that you want to be at the top of a new page.

 You can find more information on this command in Chapter 6 of *1-2-3 For Dummies*.

/Worksheet Status

Displays information about the current worksheet environment. This command is usually used to find out how much memory is available and to find out what cell is causing a circular reference (the CIRC indicator appears at the bottom of the screen).

/Worksheet Titles

Freezes rows at the top of the screen or columns at the left of the screen. If you have a large worksheet that has column headings and or row labels, this command can keep those headings and labels visible as you scroll through the worksheet.

Choose the following commands and enter the data that 1-2-3 asks you for:

Both	Freezes columns above the cell pointer and freezes rows to the left of the cell pointer.
Horizontal	Freezes rows above the cell pointer.
Vertical	Freezes columns to the left of the cell pointer.
Clear	Clears any frozen rows or columns (perhaps this should be called *Thaw*).

More stuff

 When you have frozen rows or columns, you won't be able to move the cell pointer into these areas using the normal arrow keys. However, if you really need to get there, you can use the F5 (GoTo) key to get the cell pointer into a frozen area. At the prompt, just type in a cell reference, such as **A1**.

 /Worksheet Window

/Worksheet Window

Splits the screen into two windows. This command is useful if you want to be able to see two different parts of a worksheet that normally do not fit on a single screen.

Choose the following commands and enter the data that 1-2-3 asks you for:

Horizontal	Splits the screen into two horizontal windows, based on the position of the cell pointer.
Vertical	Splits the screen into two vertical windows, based on the position of the cell pointer.
Sync	Causes scrolling in the two windows to occur together (synchronized). This is the normal setting.
Unsync	Turns off synchronized scrolling so you can scroll through one window without changing the view in the other one.
Clear	Gets you out of this two-window mode.

/Worksheet Titles

 You can find more information on this command in Chapter 5 of
1-2-3 For Dummies.

Part III:
The Wysiwyg
Command Reference

If you never intend to run 1-2-3 with the Wysiwyg add-in attached, you will have no use for this section. But if you use a Wysiwyg add-in all the time, or just on special occasions, here's where you'll find the lowdown on the Wysiwyg commands. When Wysiwyg is attached, 1-2-3 takes on a dual personality (some call it a personality disorder). Pressing the / (slash) key continues to bring up the normal menu, but pressing : (colon) calls up the completely independent Wysiwyg menu.

:Display Commands

These commands deal with how information is displayed on your screen.

:Display Colors

Customizes the Wysiwyg display in a number of ways. If you want your entire worksheet to have a yellow background, setting the background color globally is much easier than doing each cell separately.

Choose the following commands and enter the data 1-2-3 asks you for:

Background	Sets the color for the background.
Text	Sets the color for text.
Unprot	Sets the color for unprotected cells.
Cell-Pointer	Sets the color for the cell pointer.
Grid	Sets the color for the grid lines in the worksheet.
Frame	Sets the color for the worksheet frame (the thing with the row numbers and column letters).
Neg	Sets the color for negative numbers. Accountant types, for example, like to see negative numbers in red.
Lines	Sets the color for borders you draw around cells or ranges.
Shadow	Sets the color for drop shadows.
Replace	Lets you change one or more of the eight colors. 1-2-3 asks which color you want to replace, and you must enter a color number (or use the arrow keys). Press Enter to see what the replaced color looks like.
Quit	Gets you out of this menu.

If you use the **:D**isplay **C**olor **R**eplace command, you can end up with some very ugly colors, because everything with the old color is replaced with the new color.

:Display Default

Creates new default settings for Wysiwyg (or returns the settings to default values). If you find yourself adjusting the display settings every time you run 1-2-3, updating the defaults to your preferences only makes sense.

Choose the following commands and enter the data that 1-2-3 asks you for:

Restore   Replaces all the current display settings with the default values.

Update   Replaces the default display settings with the current settings that you changed.

More stuff

Using this command saves the settings you specify in the **:D**isplay menu, as well as the settings in the **:P**rint **C**onfig **P**rinter and **:P**rint **C**onfig **I**nterface menus.

:Display Font-Directory

Lets you select the directory on your disk that contains the Wysiwyg fonts. Most people never need to use this command. This directory normally stores the Wysiwyg directory.

:Display Mode

Lets you select between graphics display and text display. Working in text mode is much faster than working in graphics mode. So if speed is critical, you may want to work in text mode.

Choose the following commands and enter the data that 1-2-3 asks you for:

Graphics   Sets the display to graphics mode. This is the normal way of running Wysiwyg.

Text   Sets the display to text mode so it looks like Wysiwyg isn't loaded.

B&W   Sets the display to black and white graphics mode, which is useful if you're using a laptop computer and the display doesn't show the colors very well.

Color   Sets the display to color graphics mode.

More stuff

When you set the display to text mode, the Wysiwyg formatting doesn't go away. If you print from Wysiwyg, the formatting prints as you see it in graphics mode.

Things may look very different in text mode, and you can make changes to column widths and other things that will make your worksheet look bad when you return to graphics mode.

:Display Options

Through several subcommands, changes various aspects of the display. Using this command is largely a matter of personal preferences. For example, you may like the way high intensity looks, or you may prefer to see grid lines around cells.

Choose the following commands and enter the data that 1-2-3 asks you for:

Adapter   Lets you choose which type of display adapter Wysiwyg uses in graphics mode. Usually, **A**uto will do just fine.

Cell-Pointer   Changes the appearance of the cell pointer. You can choose between **S**olid and **O**utline. The choice is yours.

Frame	Lets you choose how the worksheet frame looks. You can choose from **1**-2-3 (normal), **E**nhanced (looks a bit better), **R**elief (looks three-dimensional), **S**pecial (choose from a variety of measurements), and **N**one (hides the frame). This option is fun to play around with.
Grid	Lets you choose whether the grid lines around the cells appear.
Intensity	Determines how bright the screen is (**N**ormal or **H**igh). This decision is just a matter of personal preference.
Page-Breaks	Lets you determine whether to show page breaks on the screen. Showing page breaks is useful if you want to avoid things like having one line print on a page by itself.

More stuff

Nothing you do here affects printed output.

:Display Quit

Gets you out of the **:D**isplay menu and puts you back in 1-2-3's READY mode.

:Display Rows

Lets you choose how many rows to display. Simply enter a number between 16 and 60. The more lines you display, the narrower the rows are. Also, you probably won't be able to read the text if you specify too many rows.

:Display Zoom

Changes the size of the display. Zooming out can give you a bird's eye view of your worksheet. On the other hand, zooming in gives you a close-up look.

Choose the following commands and enter the data that 1-2-3 asks you for:

Tiny	Shows the worksheet at 63 percent of normal size.
Small	Shows the worksheet at 87 percent of normal size.
Normal	Shows the worksheet at normal size.
Large	Shows the worksheet at 125 percent of normal size.
Huge	Shows the worksheet at 150 percent of normal size.
Manual	Lets you set the zoom percent anywhere from 25 percent to a whopping 400 percent of normal size.

More stuff

The zoom percent you set here has no effect on how large or small the type is when you print it.

Zooming out is useful if you're showing your work to a group of people gathered around your screen and you don't want them getting too close and fogging up your monitor with their breath.

:**P**rint **L**ayout **C**ompression

You can find more information on this command in Chapter 10 of *1-2-3 For Dummies.*

:Format Commands

These command let you change how cells or ranges look on screen and when printed. You may use these a lot.

:Format Bold

Sets or removes boldface for a cell or range. Boldfacing part of a worksheet (titles, for example) makes it stand out.

Choose the following commands and enter the data that 1-2-3 asks you for:

Set   Makes the selection bold.

Clear   Makes the selection not bold.

More stuff

There's a SmartIcon to turn bold on and off for an entire cell or range.

 If you just want part of a cell to be bold, edit the cell by pressing the F2 key. Move the cursor to the spot where you want bold to start and press Ctrl-A and B. Then move the cursor to where you want bold to end. Press Ctrl-E and B.

 You can find more information on this command in Chapter 10 of *1-2-3 For Dummies.*

:Format Color

Sets the color of a cell or range for display on-screen and for printing (if you happen to have a color printer). Using different colors can make seeing what various parts of your worksheet do very easy. For example, you can make all your input cells a different color so it's very clear what the user can and cannot change.

Choose the following commands and enter the data that 1-2-3 asks you for:

Text	Sets the color for the text contained in the cells.
Background	Sets the color for the background of the cells.
Negative	Sets the color for negative values.
Reverse	Reverses the colors used for text and background.
Quit	Gets you out of the menu.

More stuff

There's a SmartIcon for this command.

You can also change the colors of individual characters within a cell. Edit the cell and move the cursor to the spot where you want to change the color. Press Ctrl-A and then enter one of the following codes: **1c** (default color), **2c** (red), **3c** (green), **4c** (dark blue), **5c** (cyan), **6c** (yellow), **7c** (magenta), or **8c** (reversed colors). This new color is in effect until the end of the text, or until you decide to change the colors again. You can insert as many of these color code sequences as you want and even make every letter a different color.

It's very easy to get carried away here and create some nasty looking worksheets.

:**D**isplay **C**olors

You can find more information on this command in Chapter 10 of *1-2-3 For Dummies.*

:Format Font

Lets you set the font for a cell or range. Your worksheets can have more impact and be easier to read if you use different fonts for different parts of the worksheet. For example, you may want to put table titles in a larger font.

Choose the following commands and enter the data that 1-2-3 asks you for:

1 to **8**	Lets you choose one of the eight defined fonts from the current font set.
Replace	Replaces one of the eight defined fonts in the current font set with another available font.
Default	Changes the default font set. This command has two options. **R**estore replaces the current font set with the default font set. **U**pdate saves the current font set as the default font set.
Library	Lets you work with font libraries (AFS files). If you don't know what you're doing, using this command can quickly get very confusing.

More stuff

You can change the font within a single cell by pressing Ctrl-A and a code (**1f**, **2f**, and so on up to **8f**). But I can't think of a single reason why you would ever want to do this. So you can disregard this tip.

It's easy to go overboard on fonts. A general rule of thumb is to use no more than two or three different fonts in a worksheet.

You can find more information on this command in Chapter 10 of *1-2-3 For Dummies*.

:Format Italics

Sets or removes italics for a cell or range. Italics, like bold, is often used to make part of a worksheet stand out.

Choose the following commands and enter the data that 1-2-3 asks you for:

Set	Makes the selection italics.
Clear	Makes the selection not italics.

More stuff

There's a SmartIcon to turn italics on and off for an entire cell or range.

 If you just want part of a cell to be italics, edit the cell by pressing the F2 key. Move the cursor to the position where you want italics to start and press Ctrl-A and I. Then move the cursor to where you want italic to end. Press Ctrl-E and I.

 You can find more information on this command in Chapter 10 of *1-2-3 For Dummies.*

:*Format Lines*

Lets you draw lines around cells or ranges. Putting borders around parts of your worksheet makes it easy to see that these cells belong together. It's also useful for underlining grand totals and things such as that.

Choose the following commands and enter the data that 1-2-3 asks you for:

Outline	Draws an outline around a cell or range of cells.
Left	Draws a line along the left edge or a cell or range.
Right	Draws a line along the right edge of a cell or range.
Top	Draws a line along the top edge of a cell or range.
Bottom	Draws a line along the bottom edge of a cell or range.
All	Draws a box around each cell in the range.
Double	Draws double lines. You have to choose from a submenu to indicate where you want the double lines drawn: **O**utline, **L**eft, **R**ight, **T**op, **B**ottom, **A**ll.
Wide	Draws wide lines. You have to choose from a submenu to indicate where you want the wide lines drawn: **O**utline, **L**eft, **R**ight, **T**op, **B**ottom, **A**ll.
Clear	Removes any lines you have drawn in the range.
Shadow	Adds or removes a drop shadow from a cell or range.

 It's easy to get carried away and put borders around everything. So go easy, OK?

:Format Underline

You can find more information on this command in Chapter 10 of *1-2-3 For Dummies*.

:Format Quit

Gets you out of the :Format menu and returns you to 1-2-3's READY mode.

:Format Reset

Removes all formatting from a cell or range. Using this command is a fast way to return a cell or range back to its normal state. It also sets the font to Font-1.

More stuff

There's a SmartIcon to do the same thing.

:Format Shade

Adds or removes a shaded background to a cell or range. Shading a cell or range is yet another way to make it stand out. People often use shading for the row and column titles in a table.

Choose the following commands and enter the data that 1-2-3 asks you for:

Light   Adds light shading.

Dark   Adds dark shading.

Solid   Adds solid black shading.

Clear   Removes any shading you added.

More stuff

There's a SmartIcon that adds or removes shading.

 Use solid black shading to create very thick borders. Format the cells as **S**olid and then adjust the row height and column width to make it look like a thick border.

:Format Underline

Sets or removes underlining to text in a cell or range. Underlining can make a cell or range stand out. Using a double underline for a "bottom line" type of result is customary.

Choose the following commands and enter the data that 1-2-3 asks you for:

Single   Adds a single underline.

Double   Adds a double underline.

Wide   Adds a wide underline.

Clear   Clears any underlining that you added.

 :Format Lines

:Graph Commands

The :**G**raph command is your one-stop shopping place when you're in the market for inserting or modifying a graph or making a drawing.

:Graph Add

Adds an existing graph to the worksheet. This command lets you insert a graph right next to its data. It also lets you insert a clip art image to add more pizzazz to your worksheet.

Choose the following commands and enter the data that 1-2-3 asks you for:

Current   Inserts the current graph in the range you specify.

Named   Inserts a named graph in the range you specify. Select a graph from the list shown.

PIC   Inserts a graph saved in a PIC file in the range you specify. Select the file from the list shown.

Metafile   Inserts a CGM file in the range you specify. There's lots of clip art saved in CGM files.

Blank   Inserts a blank graph in the range you specify. Use this command if you want to set aside some space for a graph that you'll be creating later.

More stuff

The graph will be sized to fit into the range that you specify. If you change the row height or column width for an area that contains a graph, the size of the graph will adjust accordingly.

There's a SmartIcon that does this.

Although judicious use of clip art can add to a worksheet, many people overuse it and end up looking foolish.

You can find more information on this command in Chapter 10 of *1-2-3 For Dummies*.

:Graph Compute

Updates all graphs in the worksheet. Use this command if the numbers have changed and you want the graphs to show the changes. This command also reads from disk any PIC or CGM files that you inserted before.

:Graph Edit

Lets you modify an existing graph in many ways. If you're not satisfied with the way a graph looks, you can change it with these commands.

Choose the following commands and enter the data that 1-2-3 asks you for:

Add	Adds any of several items to a graph (first choose the graph). It leads to another menu with options for the type of item to add: **T**ext, **L**ine, **P**olygon, **A**rrow, **R**ectangle, **E**llipse, or **F**reehand.
Color	Lets you choose a color for several parts of the graph (including objects that you added). It leads to another menu with the following options: **L**ines, **I**nside, **T**ext, **M**ap, and **B**ackground.
Edit	Lets you change, or edit, objects that you added to the graph. It leads to another menu with the following choices: **T**ext, **C**entering, **F**ont, **L**ine-Style, **W**idth, **A**rrowheads, **S**moothing.
Options	This command has three subcommands: **G**rid (turns grid lines on or off), **C**ursor (changes the size of the graph cursor), and **F**ont-Magnification (changes the size of all text in a graph).
Quit	Gets you out of this menu and returns you to 1-2-3's READY mode.

Rearrange	Rearranges objects that you added to a graph. It leads to another menu with the following options: **D**elete, **R**estore, **M**ove, **C**opy, **L**ock, **U**nlock, **F**ront, and **B**ack.
Select	Lets you choose a bunch of objects to act upon with other command in the **:G**raph **E**dit menu. Your choices are: **O**ne, **A**ll, **N**one, **M**ore/Less, **C**ycle, **G**raph, and **Q**uit.
Transform	Changes the size or orientation of selected objects in the graph. It leads to another menu with the following options: **S**ize, **R**otate, **Q**uarter-Turn, **X**-Flip, **Y**-Flip, **H**orizontal, **V**ertical, and **C**lear.
View	Lets you choose what part of the graph to view. This command leads to another menu with these choices: **F**ull, **I**n, **P**an, **+**, **-**, **U**p, **D**own, **L**eft, and **R**ight.

More stuff

To use these commands, you must choose what you want to work with. You can do this either before you issue the command or afterward.

Note that you cannot change things about the graph elements themselves. For example, you can't use this command to change the colors of the bars in a bar chart. You have to use the /**G**raph commands to do this.

These commands do a lot of things. The best way to learn about them is to dig in, play around, and see what happens.

:Graph Goto

Moves the cell pointer to the upper left worksheet cell that contains a graph. If you have an assortment of graphs inserted, this is an easy way to find the one you want.

More stuff

After you issue this command, you need to choose the graph from a list of all graphs.

:Graph Move

Moves a graph on the worksheet to a different location. Using this command is the only way to move a graph on a worksheet (short of deleting it and adding it again in a different spot).

More stuff

You must choose the graph to move by moving the cell pointer to the graph and then indicate the upper left cell where you want to move it to.

:Graph Quit

Gets you out of the **:G**raph menu and returns you to 1-2-3's READY mode.

:Graph Remove

Deletes a graph from the worksheet. Using this command is the only way to get rid of a graph on a worksheet.

More stuff

After you issue this command, you specify the graph that you want to zap. The graph is still available, so you can insert it again at some other time. You will, however, lose any editing that you did to it with the **:G**raph **E**dit command.

:Graph Settings

Lets you change several settings for graphs in a worksheet. Using this command gives you more control over how a graph looks and also lets you change its size.

Choose the following commands and enter the data that 1-2-3 asks you for:

Graph   Replaces an existing graph with another one. After you issue this command, you can choose the graph (or a PIC or CGM file).

Range   Changes the size of the graph by changing the range that it fits in.

Sync   Determines whether the graph is updated automatically if its data is changed.

Display   Lets you turn off the display of a graph if you find that it's slowing things down too much. It's still there (and will print) — it just doesn't show up on-screen.

Opaque   Lets you determine whether you can see the underlying cell contents through the graph.

Making a graph transparent with the opaque option is an easy way to "add" text to a graph (but if you move the graph with the **:G**raph **M**ove command, the underlying text won't come with it).

You can find more information on this command in Chapter 10 of *1-2-3 For Dummies.*

:Graph View

Displays a graph saved as a PIC file or a CGM file. You use this command mainly to preview graphic files before you insert them into a worksheet with the **:G**raph **A**dd command.

Choose the following commands and enter the data that 1-2-3 asks you for:

PIC	Lets you choose a PIC file to view.
Metafile	Lets you choose a CGM file to view.

:Graph Add

You can find more information on this command in Chapter 10 of *1-2-3 For Dummies.*

:Graph Zoom

Displays a graph using the full screen. The only way to see a graph in all its glory — filling up the whole screen — is to use this command. Unlike the **/G**raph **V**iew command, this command also shows any editing you did with the **:G**raph **E**dit command.

More stuff

After issuing this command, you must choose a graph from the worksheet by moving the cell pointer to it.

:Named-Style

Formats a cell or range using a named style. Using named styles is a great way to go and is much easier than doing individual formatting for cells or ranges.

Choose the following commands and enter the data that 1-2-3 asks you for:

1 to **8**	Applies the specified style number to the selection.
Define	Lets you change a style.

More stuff

1-2-3 doesn't have any preset named styles. You have to define
your own in order to use any.

If you use the **:N**amed-Style **D**efine command to change an
existing named style, every cell that's tagged with that style will
change. Actually, this feature is a real benefit. You can easily
make mass formatting changes simply by redefining a style.

You can find more information on this command in Chapter 10 of
1-2-3 For Dummies.

:Print Commands

These commands involve printing with Wysiwyg formatting. When you press **:P**rint, 1-2-3 displays a window that shows all the current settings. Using this window is much easier than going through all the menus.

Printing in Wysiwyg is completely independent of printing through the normal 1-2-3 menus. For example, if you choose a print range using the **/P**rint command, the Wysiwyg **:P**rint command won't know about it. Also, if you use the normal **/P**rint command with a worksheet that has Wysiwyg formatting, the formatting won't print. You have to use the **:P**rint command to get the formatting to show.

:Print Background

Sends your Wysiwyg-formatted worksheet to an encoded file and then prints it in the background so you can continue working away.

More stuff

This command works by creating a file on disk that holds the stuff to be printed. Therefore, 1-2-3 asks you for a filename to hold the printed output before it sends your file to the printer. It automatically adds the ENC extension. You still have to go through the normal **:P**rint commands in order to tell 1-2-3 what you want printed.

If you have a lot of printing to do, this command lets you continue working while the printing is being done. Printing from Wysiwyg usually takes much longer than normal 1-2-3 printing.

 In order to do background printing, you must have run the BPRINT program before you started 1-2-3. You cannot use the **/S**ystem command to do this.

:Print Config

Changes some of the options used in printing. There may be times when you need to print to a different printer, or you may add a new cartridge, want to change the paper orientation, or other things like this.

Choose the following commands and enter the data that 1-2-3 asks you for:

1st-Cart	Lets you specify the first font cartridge your printer has (if appropriate).
2nd-Cart	Lets you specify the second font cartridge your printer has (if appropriate).
Bin	Lets you choose which bin the printer should get its paper from (if appropriate).
Interface	Lets you specify **S**erial or **P**arallel.
Orientation	Lets you choose either **P**ortrait (vertical) or Landscape (horizontal) printing orientation.
Printer	Lets you choose the printer from a list of installed printers.
Quit	Gets you out of this menu and returns you to the **:P**rint menu.

More stuff

This information is shown also in the print settings window. Using this window is much easier than using the commands.

 If you change printers, make sure that the printer is actually available. Otherwise, you may end up with pages full of weird characters.

:Print File

Creates a special encoded file that contains everything that would normally be sent to a printer (including all the cryptic printer-specific codes).

More stuff

1-2-3 asks you for a filename to hold the printed output before it sends you file to the printer. It automatically adds the ENC extension.

This command can be handy if you don't have a printer hooked up (which is common for laptop users on an airplane). You can store in a file what you would normally print. Then, when you get to a place that has a printer, you can copy the file to the printer, and the output looks just like it would have looked if you had the printer on the plane with you. The DOS command to do this is

```
COPY filename.ENC PRN
```

The encoded file that's produced is for the printer that you have installed in 1-2-3. If you try to copy this file to a different printer, the results will probably be garbage.

:Print Go

Starts printing.

More stuff

There's a SmartIcon to start printing.

:Print Info

Displays or removes the print status information that tells you everything you need to know about the print job you're setting up. The print status screen is very handy, but it covers up virtually all your worksheet. If you want to peek at what's underneath, you can hide the status screen with this command.

:Print Layout

Lets you change lots of things regarding how your printed output will look.

Choose the following commands and enter the data that 1-2-3 asks you for:

Borders
Lets you specify or change the row and column borders that print on each page. It leads to another menu: **T**op (choose the rows), **L**eft (choose the columns), **C**lear (removes all borders), and **Q**uit (return to the :**P**rint **L**ayout menu).

Compression
Lets you decide whether to compress the output. It has two choices: **M**anual (you specify a compression percentage) or **A**utomatic (you let 1-2-3 figure out the compression percentage so your worksheet fits on one page).

Default
Lets you load in the default page layout settings or save the current settings as new defaults.

Library
Lets you choose from other page layouts that are stored on your disk.

Margins
Lets you change any of the margins on the page.

Page-Size
Lets you tell 1-2-3 what size paper you are using. Choosing this command leads to a menu with eight paper size choices.

Titles
Lets you specify a header and/or footer that appears on every page.

More stuff

This information is shown also in the print settings window. Using this window is much easier than using the commands.

:Print Preview

Displays a spitting image of the printed output on your screen. Because Wysiwyg printing can take a long time, this option lets you make sure you're getting what you think you're getting.

:Print Quit

Gets you out of this menu and returns you to 1-2-3's READY mode.

:Print Range

Lets you set or clear the range to be printed (you have to tell 1-2-3 what you want to print). It's also useful for clearing a print range that you set earlier.

Choose the following commands and enter the data that 1-2-3 asks you for:

Set   Lets you choose the range that you want to print. Even if you want to print everything, you still need to specify the print range.

Clear   Clears the existing print range.

You can find more information on this command in Chapter 10 of *1-2-3 For Dummies.*

:Print Settings

Controls lots of things that determine how the printing goes. This command is handy if you need to print only part of a print range, don't like to see grid lines, want more than one copy, or want to specify the starting page number.

Choose the following commands and enter the data that 1-2-3 asks you for:

Begin   Lets you specify the first page to print.

Copies   Lets you specify how many copies you want to print.

End   Lets you specify the last page to print.

Frame   Lets you specify whether to print the worksheet frame.

Grid   Lets you specify whether to print the grid lines between cells.

Quit   Gets you out of this menu.

Reset   Restores all the default settings for this menu.

Start-Number   Lets you tell 1-2-3 what the first page number should be.

Wait   Lets you specify whether you want the printer to pause between pages or not.

More stuff

Most of this information is shown also in the print settings window. Using this window is much easier than using the commands.

:Quit

Gets you out of the Wysiwyg menu and returns you to 1-2-3's READY mode.

:Special Commands

These commands are used for copying, moving, importing, or exporting Wysiwyg formats.

:Special Copy

Copies formats from one location to another. If you spend several minutes getting a cell or range formatted just right, you can repeat all this formatting somewhere else by using the :Special Copy command. It copies only the formats, not the contents, of the cell.

More stuff

The normal /Copy command also copies Wysiwyg formats.

The :Special Copy command works very similarly to the normal /Copy command. For example, you can copy one cell's formatting to another cell or to a whole range.

When you copy Wysiwyg formats, the old formats in the area that you're copying them to are completely replaced. For example, if something is already italic and you copy to it new formatting that doesn't include italic, the italic formatting goes away.

:Special Move

:Special Export

Saves the Wysiwyg formatting in the current worksheet to a FMT or ALL file. The ALL files are used with the Allways add-in (a precursor to Wysiwyg).

More stuff

This command doesn't save any data — just formats.

If you have a bunch of worksheets that you want to look the same, you can format one and then save the formatting in an FMT file. You can then apply these saved formats to your other files with the :Special Import command.

:Special Import

:Special Import

Brings in Wysiwyg formatting from a file stored on disk and applies it to the current worksheet. It can import FMT or ALL files. The ALL files are created by the Allways add-in (what some people used before Wysiwyg was available).

Choose the following commands and enter the data that 1-2-3 asks you for:

All   Replaces all formatting (formats, named styles, graphics) in the current worksheet with formatting from the FMT or ALL files.

Named-Styles   Replaces only the named styles in the current worksheet.

Fonts   Replaces only the font set in the current worksheet.

Graphs   Adds all the graphics to the current worksheet.

More stuff

This command doesn't import any data — just formats.

:Special Export

:Special Move

Moves Wysiwyg formats from one area of a worksheet to another. If you find that you accidentally formatted the wrong range with all sorts of fancy formatting, you can use this command to move the formats to the right spot.

More stuff

The normal /**M**ove command also move the Wysiwyg formats along with the cell contents.

When you move Wysiwyg formats, the old formats in the area that you're moving them to are completely replaced. For example, if something is already bold and you move new formatting to it that doesn't include bold, the bold formatting goes away.

:**S**pecial **C**opy

:Text Commands

The commands in this menu let your work with a range of labels as paragraphs. When you do something with these commands, the cells take on a special text alignment attribute. The word {Text} appears in the edit line when you move the cell pointer over the cell.

:Text Align

Changes the alignment of labels in a range. Using this command is a fast way to change how a bunch of labels look with only a single command. It's very useful for centering labels over a group of columns (as in the title of a table).

Choose the following commands and enter the data that 1-2-3 asks you for:

Left	Changes the alignment to left justified.
Right	Changes the alignment to right justified.
Center	Changes the alignment to centered.
Even	Changes the alignment to even (flush left and flush right).

More stuff

This command is much more versatile than the normal **/R**ange Label command. When you're aligning text, you can specify additional columns, and the text is aligned over the entire column range.

If you use **L**eft or **C**enter alignment, your worksheet will often look like the text is in a different cell. But if you move the cell pointer around and look at the edit line, you'll see that the text is actually in the first column of the range.

:Text Clear

Clears the special text alignment attribute from a cell or a range so 1-2-3 no longer treats these cells as a text range. Use this command if you want to return text that has been aligned with one of the :Text Align commands back to normal.

 :Text Set

:Text Edit

Lets you edit a range of labels as a single unit, turning a range of your worksheet into a mini word processor. This command is useful for entering or editing a block of text. After you specify the range for the text to be edited, you can use the arrow keys to jump up and down lines, much like you would in a word processor.

More stuff

When you select the range, choose as many rows and columns as you need to display the text. If you enter too much text, 1-2-3 tells you that the input range is full. If you get this message, reissue the command and specify a larger range.

:Text Reformat

Reformats a group of labels so they fit nicely into a range you specify. If you have a group of labels in a worksheet that you use for instructions or to provide explanatory information, this command lets you easily change the text and then reformat the whole works so it looks good and aligned.

More stuff

This command is very similar to the **/R**ange **J**ustify command.

:Text Set

Sets the special text alignment attribute for a cell or range. When you choose a command like **:T**ext **A**lign, the text alignment attribute is set automatically (so you won't have to use this command).

:Worksheet Commands

These commands let you change row heights and column widths and insert manual page breaks.

:Worksheet Column

Changes the width of a column or group of column.

Choose the following commands and enter the data that 1-2-3 asks you for:

Set-Width   Sets the column width. 1-2-3 prompts you to choose the column or column range. Do so and press Enter. Then use the arrow keys to adjust the column width to your liking and press Enter. Or you can type in a number for the column width.

Reset-Width   Resets the column width to the global column width setting. This command works with either a single column or a group of columns.

You can find more information on this command in Chapter 10 of *1-2-3 For Dummies.*

:Worksheet Page

Lets you insert a manual page break.

Choose the following commands and enter the data that 1-2-3 asks you for:

Column   Inserts a page break at the current column.

Delete   Gets rid of a page break that you inserted.

Quit   Gets you out of this menu and returns you to 1-2-3's READY mode.

Row   Inserts a page break at the current row.

More stuff

This commands lets you specify exactly where the page breaks occur when you print. If you want the summary of each sale to start on a separate page, this is the command to use. Unlike the normal /**W**orksheet **P**age command, this one lets you specify column breaks.

There's a SmartIcon that lets you insert page breaks.

:Worksheet Row

Sets the height of one or more rows. This command is useful for inserting white space above a range. You could insert a bunch of new rows to do this, but it's sometimes easier just to change the height of one row.

Choose the following commands and enter the data that 1-2-3 asks you for:

Set-Height   Sets the height. 1-2-3 asks you to specify the rows to change. Then, use the arrow keys to adjust the height or type in a number.

Auto   Sets the row height to fit the largest text in the row.

It's possible to set the row height so that it's not deep enough, cutting off the top part of the text.

You can find more information on this command in Chapter 10 of *1-2-3 For Dummies*.

Part IV:
The Dummies Guide to
1-2-3 @Functions

1-2-3 provides a boatload of built-in functions that you can use to do special calculations and perform wizardry with labels. These are known as @functions (pronounced at-funk-shuns). They all begin with @, and most of them take arguments, which are always enclosed in parentheses and separated by commas. The arguments can be references to cells, actual numbers, or strings. When 1-2-3 "evaluates" an @function, it returns a single value or label.

This section summarizes what each of these @functions can do for you. For more information, enter the @function in 1-2-3's edit line and press the F1 key. 1-2-3 will tell you more about the @function and even give you an example.

For more background on 1-2-3's @functions, refer to Chapters 12 and 13 in *1-2-3 For Dummies*.

The Dummies Guide to 1-2-3 @Functions

@@(cell_reference)

Returns the address of *cell_reference*, as a string.

@?

Does nothing. 1-2-3 can't interpret this @function. It may appear on worksheets translated from other versions of 1-2-3.

@ABS(number)

Returns the absolute value of *number*. This @function is useful as an argument to other @functions that require a positive value.

@ACOS(x)

Returns the arccosine of *x*, which is the inverse of a cosine.

@ASIN(x)

Returns the arcsine of *x*, which is the inverse of a sine.

@ATAN(x)

Returns the arctangent of *x*, which is the inverse of the tangent.

@ATAN2(x,y)

Returns the arctangent of *y/x*.

@AVG(list)

Computes the average of a range or a list of arguments.

@CELL(attribute,range)

Returns various characteristics of a particular cell.

@CELLPOINTER(attribute)

Returns various characteristics of the cell where the cell pointer is.

@CHAR(number)

Converts a number to its equivalent Lotus International Character Set (LICS) entry.

@CHOOSE(offset,list)

Returns one value from a *list*, the position of which is determined by the value of *offset*.

@CLEAN(string)

Removes strange characters from a string. This @function is used often to clean up data imported from various sources.

@CODE(string)

Returns the LICS code corresponding to the *string*. If *string* is more than one character, it returns the LICS code of the first character.

@COLS(range)

Returns the number of columns in *range*.

@COS(x)

Returns the cosine of *x*.

@COUNT(list)

Returns the number of nonblank cells in a *list* or range.

@CTERM(interest,future_val,present_val)

Returns the number of compounding periods required for an investment (*present_val*) to reach a specified *future_val*, given a specified *interest* rate.

@DATE(year,month,day)

Returns the date serial number for *year*, *month*, and *day*.

@DATEVALUE(date_string)

Returns the date serial number of a string (*date_string*) that looks like a date.

@DAVG(input_range,offset,criteria_range)

Selects the values at the *offset* in *input_range* that meet the criteria in *criteria_range* and calculates the average.

@DAY(date)

Returns the day of the month for a serial number *date*.

@DCOUNT(input_range,offset,criteria_range)

Selects the values at the *offset* in *input_range* that meet the criteria in *criteria_range* and returns how many there are.

@DDB(cost,salvage,life,period)

Calculates the double-declining balance depreciation for a particular *period*. This value is valid for an asset of a given *cost*, given *salvage* value, given *life*, and a particular *period* in its life.

@DMAX(input_range,offset,criteria_range)

Chooses the values at the *offset* in *input_range* that meet the criteria in *criteria_range* and returns the largest value.

@DMIN(input_range,offset,criteria_range)

Chooses the values at the *offset* in *input_range* that meet the criteria in *criteria_range* and returns the smallest value.

@DSTD(input_range,offset,criteria_range)

Chooses the values at the *offset* in *input_range* that meet the criteria in *criteria_range* and calculates the standard deviation.

@DSUM(input_range,offset,criteria_range)

Chooses the values at the *offset* in *input_range* that meet the criteria in *criteria_range* and calculates their sum of them.

@DVAR(input_range,offset,criteria_range)

Chooses the values at the *offset* in *input_range* that meet the criteria in *criteria_range* and calculates the variance.

@ERR

Returns *ERR* in a cell as a signal for unacceptable numbers.

@EXACT(string1,string2)

Compares *string1* with *string2* and returns 1 if they are exactly the same and 0 if they're not.

@EXP(number)

Returns *e* to the power of *number*. (*e* is a mathematical constant approximately equal to 2.7182818.)

@FALSE

Returns a logical FALSE (0). This @function is almost always used with other @functions.

@FIND(search_string,string,start_number)

Returns the position in *string* in which *search_string* begins. Searching starts at position *start_number* in the *string*.

@FV(payment,interest,term)

Calculates the future value of an investment based on a given *payment* amount, a given *interest* rate, and a given *term* of payments.

@HLOOKUP(key,range,row_offset)

Returns the string or value in *range* that is less than or equal to
the given *key* (in the first row of the table) and is in the given
row_offset.

@HOUR(time)

Returns the hour of the day for a serial number *time*.

@IF(test,true,false)

Returns *true* if *test* evaluates to logical TRUE; otherwise, returns
false.

@INDEX(range,column,row)

Returns the string or value that's in *range* at the *column* offset and
row offset.

@INT(number)

Returns the integer part of *number* by truncating everything after
the decimal point.

@IRR(guess,cashflows)

Calculates the internal rate of return for a series of *cashflows*
stored in a range. You need to supply a *guess* to get it started.

@ISAAF(add-in_function)

Returns 1 if the named *add-in_function* is loaded; otherwise,
returns 0.

@ISAPP(add-in)

Returns 1 if the named *add-in* is loaded; otherwise, returns 0.

@ISERR(x)

Returns 1 if *x* evaluates to ERR; otherwise, it returns 0.

@ISNA(x)

Returns 1 if *x* evaluates to NA; otherwise, it returns 0.

@ISNUMBER(x)

Returns 1 if *x* evaluates to a number, blank, NA, or ERR; otherwise, it returns 0.

@ISSTRING(x)

Returns 1 if *x* evaluates to a string; otherwise, it returns 0.

@LEFT(string,digits)

Returns the left part of *string,* consisting of the first number of *digits*.

@LENGTH(string)

Returns the number of characters in *string*.

@LN(number)

Returns the natural logarithm of *number*.

@*LOG(number)*

Returns the standard logarithm of *number.*

@*LOWER(string)*

Converts all uppercase letters in *string* to lowercase.

@*MAX(list)*

Returns the largest value in *list.*

@*MID(string,start_pos,length)*

Returns a string of a *length* characters from *string,* starting at position *start_ pos.*

@*MIN(list)*

Returns the smallest value in the list.

@*MINUTE(time)*

Returns the minute of the hour for a serial number *time.*

@*MOD(number,divisor)*

Returns the remainder from a division of *number* divided by *divisor.*

@*MONTH(date)*

Returns the month for the serial number *date.*

@N(range)

Tests a *range,* which is usually a single cell, to see whether it's a number. If so, it returns the number; otherwise, it returns 0.

@NA

Returns NA. This @function is most often used in conjunction with other @functions.

@NOW

Returns the current date serial number and time serial number. This @function is updated every time the worksheet is recalculated.

@NPV(interest,cashflows)

Calculates the net present value of a series of future cash flows in a *range,* discounted at some *interest* rate.

@PI

Returns the number of π to this many places: 3.14159265358979324. Sorry, but that's as exact as it gets.

@PMT(principal,interest,term)

Calculates the periodic payment needed to repay a loan of a given *principal* amount, at a given *interest* rate, over a given *term.*

@PROPER(string)

Converts *string* into proper case. The first letter in each word is uppercase, and all other letters are lowercase.

@*PV(payment,interest,term)*

Calculates the present value of a series of equal-amount *payments* at a given *interest* rate for a given *term*.

@*RAND*

Returns a random number between 0 and 1 inclusive. A new random number is returned every time the worksheet is calculated.

@*RATE(future_value,present_value,term)*

Calculates the interest rate required for a *present_value* to reach a *future_value* in a specified *term*.

@*REPEAT(string,number)*

Repeats *string* for *number* of times. This is often used to produce crude underlining.

@*REPLACE(string,start_pos,* *length,replacement_string)*

Moves to *start_ pos* in *string* and replaces *length* letters with *replacement_string*.

@*RIGHT(string,number)*

Returns the rightmost part of *string*, consisting of the last *number* characters.

@ROUND(number,precision)

Returns a rounded version of *number*. *Precision* determines how to round it. A positive *precision* means the number of places to the right of the decimal point; a negative *precision* means the number of places to the left of the decimal. If *precision* is zero, you need to round it to an integer value.

@ROWS(range)

Returns the number of rows in *range*.

@S(range)

Tests the upper left cell in a given *range* (usually only a single cell) to see if it's a string. If so, it returns the string; otherwise, it returns an empty string ("").

@SECOND(time)

Returns the second of the minute of the hour of the day for a serial number *time*.

@SIN(x)

Returns the sin of *x*.

@SLN(cost,salvage,life)

Calculates the straight-line depreciation (an equal amount each period) for an asset of a given *cost*, with a given useful *life*, with a given *salvage* value.

@SORT(number)

Returns the square root of *number*.

@STD(list)

Returns the standard deviation of *list*.

@STRING(number,decimal_places)

Converts *number* into a string with number of decimal places equal to *decimal_ places*.

@SUM(list)

Returns the sum of all values in *list*.

@SYD(cost,salvage,life,period)

Calculates the sum-of-the-years'-digits depreciation amount for a given *period*. This is valid for an asset with a given *cost*, given *salvage* value, and a particular *period* in its *life*.

@TAN(x)

Returns the tangent of *x*.

@TERM(payment,interest,future_value)

Calculates the term required for a given *payment* at a given *interest* rate to produce a desired *future_value*.

@TIME(hour,minute,second)

Returns the time serial number for *hour, minute,* and *second.*

@TIMEVALUE(time_string)

Converts *time_string,* which looks like a time, into an actual time serial number.

@TODAY

Returns the serial number for the current date.

@TRIM(string)

Removes blank spaces from the beginning and end of *string* and also removes all series of spaces with a single space.

@TRUE

Returns a logical TRUE (1). This is almost always used with other @functions.

@UPPER(string)

Converts all the lowercase letters in *string* to uppercase.

@VALUE(string)

Converts *string,* which looks like a number, into an actual number.

@VAR(list)

Calculates the variance of the values in *list*.

@VLOOKUP(key,range,column_offset)

Returns the string or value in *range* that is less than or equal to the given *key* (in the first row of the table) and is in the given *column_offset*.

@YEAR(date)

Returns the year for a serial number *date*.

You can find more information on @functions in Chapters 12 and 13 of *1-2-3 For Dummies*.

Part V:
The Dummies Guide to
1-2-3 Macro Commands

I know, I know, the very thought of 1-2-3 macros makes you want to call in sick. Believe it or not, some people actually enjoy writing macros. For those select few, I've compiled this reference list of 1-2-3 macro commands. It starts out with macro key names and finishes off with the actual macro commands that have caused countless hours of grief.

For more about macros, look to Chapter 9 of *1-2-3 For Dummies*.

Macro Key Names

When you're writing a macro, you need some way of specifying keystrokes that you might make. For example, how do you express the concept of pressing Enter to a macro? Simple. Just use {~}. Enter is one of many keystrokes that must be accounted for in 1-2-3 macros. For those who like to know that such lists exist, this list is for you.

A macro can simulate just about any keystroke a user can make in the course of running 1-2-3. For most keystrokes, you can simply insert the key in the macro. For others, however, you need to enter them in a special way. Here's a list of how to represent keystrokes in a macro.

The Dummies Guide to Macro Key Names

~

Simulates pressing Enter.

{~}

Simulates pressing a tilde (~).

{{}

Simulates pressing a left curly bracket.

{}}

Simulates pressing a right curly bracket.

{ABS [number]}

Simulates pressing the F4 key; the optional number indicates how many times the key is pressed.

{ADDIN}

Simulates pressing Alt-F10 to invoke an add-in (and must be followed by the add-in number).

{APP1}

Simulates pressing Alt-F7 (to invoke the first add-in key).

{APP2}

Simulates pressing Alt-F8 (to invoke the second add-in key).

{APP3}

Simulates pressing Alt-F9 (to invoke the third add-in key).

{BS [number]}

Simulates pressing Backspace an optional number of times.

{BIGLEFT [number]}

Simulates pressing Shift-Tab (or Ctrl-←) an optional number of times.

{BIGRIGHT [number]}

Simulates pressing Tab (or Ctrl-→) an optional number of times.

{CALC [number]}

Simulates pressing the F9 key an optional number of times.

{DELETE [number]} or {DEL [number]}

Simulates pressing Delete an optional number of times.

{DOWN [number]} or {D [number]}

Simulates pressing ↓ an optional number of times.

{EDIT}

Simulates pressing the F2 key.

{END}

Simulates pressing End.

{ESCAPE [number]} or {ESC [number]}

Simulates pressing Esc an optional number of times.

{GOTO}

Simulates pressing the F5 key.

[GRAPH]

Simulates pressing the F10 key.

[HELP]

Simulates pressing the F1 key.

[HOME]

Simulates pressing Home.

[INSERT] or [INS]

Simulates pressing Insert.

[LEFT [number]] or [L [number]]

Simulates pressing ← an optional number of times.

[MENU]

Simulates pressing the / (slash) key.

[NAME [number]]

Simulates pressing the F3 key an optional number of times.

[PGDN [number]]

Simulates pressing PgDn an optional number of times.

[PGUP [number]]

Simulates pressing PgUp an optional number of times.

[QUERY]

Simulates pressing the F7 key.

[RIGHT [number]] or *[R [number]]*

Simulates pressing → an optional number of times.

[TABLE]

Simulates pressing the F8 key.

[UP [number]] or *[U [number]]*

Simulates pressing ↑ an optional number of times.

[WINDOW]

Simulates pressing the F6 key.

Macro Commands

When a macro is being executed, 1-2-3 interprets all the keystrokes (just described) as well as the special macro commands (described next). If you don't understand this stuff, don't worry about it. If you do understand this stuff, the following list may be handy.

The Dummies Guide to Commands

{?}

Pauses the macro to accept keyboard input from the user.

{APPENDBELOW destination,source}

Adds the *source* range directly below the *destination* range.

{APPENDRIGHT destination,source}

Adds the *source* range directly to the right of the *destination* range.

{BEEP [tone_number]}

Makes a beep using *tone_number*, which can range from 1 to 4.

{BLANK location}

Erases the contents of *location*.

{BORDERSOFF}

Turns the worksheet frame off.

{BORDERSON}

Turns the worksheet frame back on.

{BRANCH location}

Makes the macro execution continue at *location*.

{BREAK}

Stops the macro and returns 1-2-3 to READY mode.

{BREAKOFF}

Keeps the program from recognizing a user's attempt to stop a macro by pressing Ctrl-Break.

{BREAKON}

Cancels {BREAKOFF} so the macro can be stopped if the user presses Ctrl-Break.

{CLOSE}

Closes a text file that a macro opened.

{CONTENTS destination,source, *[width],[format]}*

Copies the contents of *source* to *destination* and stores it as a label. These two arguments must be a single cell. The two optional arguments change the cell width and label format of the source cell; without these arguments the width and format of the destination cell are the same as the source cell.

{DEFINE loc1[:type1],...,locN[:typeN]}

Stores arguments that you want to pass to a macro subroutine.

{DISPATCH location}

Sends macro execution (control) to a new *location*.

{FILESIZE location}

Determines how large the current text file opened by a macro is and puts the answer in *location*.

{FOR counter,start,stop, *step,subroutine}*

Starts a macro loop by executing *subroutine*. *Counter* keeps track of the times through the loop, *start* is the starting count, *stop* is the ending count, and *step* is the increment value for the count.

{FORBREAK}

Cancels a loop started by a {FOR} instruction.

{FORM input,[call_table], [include_keys],[exclude_keys]}

Stops a macro temporarily so the user can enter data into a form; the optional arguments specify ranges.

{FORMBREAK}

Stops a {FORM} command.

{FRAMEOFF}

Turns off the worksheet frame.

{FRAMEON}

Turns the worksheet frame back on.

{GET location}

Stops a macro to get a single keystroke from the user and stores it in *location*.

{GETLABEL prompt,location}

Stops a macro to get a label from the user and prompts with *prompt*. The label is stored in *location*.

{GETNUMBER prompt,location}

Stops a macro to get a value from the user and prompts with *prompt*. The value is stored in *location*.

{GETPOS location}

Gets the current cell pointer position and stores it in *location*.

{GRAPHOFF}

Removes a graph displayed by the {GRAPHON} command.

{GRAPHON [named_graph],[nodisplay]}

Shows a graph (or simply makes a set of graph settings the current graph); the optional arguments name the graph (other than the current graph) and specify whether it is displayed.

{IF condition}

Executes the remaining macro commands in the cell only if *condition* is true.

{INDICATE [string]}

Changes the 1-2-3 mode indicator to *string*.

{LET location,expression}

Puts *expression* (a value or label) into the worksheet at *location*.

{LOOK location}

Checks to see whether the user has made any keystrokes while the macro was running and stores them in *location*.

{MENUBRANCH location}

Displays a custom menu defined at *location*.

{MENUCALL location}

Displays a custom menu by calling a subroutine at *location*.

{ONERROR branch,[message]}

Branches to a macro routine when an error has occurred.

{OPEN filename,access_mode}

Opens a text file named *filename* with read and write access determined by *access_mode*.

{PANELOFF [clear]}

Turns off updating of the control panel (to speed things up).

{PANELON}

Turns on updating of the control panel (the normal way of doing things).

{PUT range,col,row,value}

Puts a *value* or label in *range*. You can also specify a *col* offset or *row* offset from *location*.

{QUIT}

Stops the macro and puts 1-2-3 back in READY mode.

{READ bytecount,location}

Reads *bytecount* characters from the open text file and stores them in *location*.

{READLN location}

Reads a whole line from the open text file and stores it in *location*.

{RECALC location,
[condition],[iterations]}

Recalculates the formulas in *location* row by row; the optional arguments specify true/false conditions and the number of times you want the recalculation done — if you use one, you have to use the other.

{RECALCCOL location,
[condition],[iterations]}

Recalculates the formulas in *location* column by column.

{RESTART}

Clears information used by subroutines.

{RETURN}

Returns the macro execution to the instruction following the last subroutine call.

{SETPOS file_position}

Moves the file pointer to *file_position* in the open text file.

{SUBROUTINE [arg1],[arg2],...,[argN]}

Calls the macro *subroutine* with optional arguments that are numbers or strings.

{SYSTEM command}

Executes a DOS *command* (which must be in quotations — up to 123 characters).

{WAIT argument}

Pauses the macro until the time specified in *argument*.

{WINDOWSOFF}

Turns off windows updating while a macro is running (to speed things up).

{WINDOWSON}

Turns windows updating back on (the normal condition).

{WRITE string}

Puts *string* into the open text file.

{WRITELN string}

Puts *string* into the open text file and also inserts carriage return and line feed characters.

You can find more information on macros in Chapter 9 of *1-2-3 For Dummies.*

Part VI:
The Dummies Guide to
1-2-3 Keys

At any given time, pressing a specific key in 1-2-3 can have a major impact on what happens in your worksheet. Often, the effect of pressing a key varies depending on the mode that 1-2-3 is in. This section gives you exhaustive lists of what the various keys do under various circumstances:

- The function keys are the keys or key combinations that have 1-2-3 functions assigned to them — they all use the letter *F* in combination with a number from 1 to 10!

- The cursor movement keys are the ones you use to get around in the worksheet.

- The EDIT mode keys are active when you're editing the contents of a cell. 1-2-3 displays EDIT in the upper left corner or your screen.

- The MENU mode keys are active when you're in the 1-2-3 menu. 1-2-3 displays MENU in the upper left corner of your screen. These keys do pretty much what you would expect.

The Dummies Guide to 1-2-3 Function Keys

F1 (Help)

Calls up 1-2-3's online help system.

F2 (Edit)

Lets you edit the current cell.

F3 (Name)

Displays a list of range names for you to choose from.

F4 (Absolute)

Cycles through all the possible types of cell references (absolute, relative, mixed) when you're editing a cell.

F5 (GoTo)

Lets you quickly move the cell pointer to a place you want to be.

F6 (Window)

Switches between two displayed windows.

F7 (Query)

Repeats the last query you did when working with a database.

F8 (Table)

Repeats the last /Data Table command you issued.

F9 (Calc)

Recalculate all the formulas in your worksheet if you have recalculation set to manual. Use this key only if the CALC indicator appears at the bottom of your screen.

F10 (Graph)

Displays the current graph using the whole screen.

Alt-F1 (Compose)

Lets you compose a special character that's not on your keyboard.

Alt-F2 (Step)

Toggles STEP mode (one command at a time) when you're running a macro.

Alt-F3 (Run)

Runs a macro.

Alt-F4 (Undo)

Often cancels the effects of what you just did if Undo is enabled.

Alt-F5 (Learn)

Starts macro recording.

Alt-F6 (Zoom)

Makes the current window fill up the whole screen if you have two windows displayed.

Alt-F7 (App1)

Activates the add-in you assigned to the first add-in key.

Alt-F8 (App2)

Activates the add-in you assigned to the second add-in key.

Alt-F9 (App3)

Activates the add-in you assigned to the third add-in key.

Alt-F10 (Addin)

Activates the add-in you assigned to the fourth add-in key — or activates the add-in menu if nothing is assigned to the fourth add-in key.

The Dummies Guide to 1-2-3 Movement Keys

Ctrl- ←

Moves the cell pointer one screen to the left in the same row.

Ctrl- →

Moves the cell pointer one screen to the right in the same row. (Same as Tab.)

##

Moves the cell pointer one cell down. (Same as Tab.)

End

Does nothing by itself. After pressing End, press an arrow key (←, →, ↑, ↓) to move to the end of the current block (or to the first occupied cell).

End-Home

Moves the cell pointer to the last column and the last row of the worksheet. Press End first and then Home.

Home

Moves the cell pointer to cell A1.

Moves the cell pointer one cell to the left.

PgDn

Moves the cell pointer down 20 rows in the same column.

PgUp

Moves the cell pointer up 20 rows in the same column.

Moves the cell pointer one cell to the right.

Shift-Tab

Moves the cell pointer one screen to the left in the same row. (Same as Ctrl-←.)

Tab

Moves the cell pointer one screen to the right in the same row. (Same as Ctrl-→.)

Moves the cell pointer one cell up.

The Dummies Guide to 1-2-3 EDIT Mode Keys

Backspace

Deletes the character to the left of the cursor.

Ctrl- ←

Ends editing and moves the cell pointer one screen to the left in the same row. (Same as Shift-Tab.)

Ctrl- →

Ends editing and moves the cell pointer one screen to the right in the same row. (Same as Tab.)

Delete

Deletes the character at the cursor.

##

Ends editing and moves the cell pointer one cell down.

End

Moves the cursor to the last character in the cell you're editing.

Enter

Ends editing and leaves the cell pointer where it is.

Escape

Lets you bail out of editing a cell without causing anything to change.

F2

Switches among different edit modes. The exact behavior of this key depends on what's in the edit line. It's most useful for getting into POINT mode if you want to point to a cell or range while editing.

F9

Converts a formula to a value.

Home

Moves the cursor to the first character in the cell you're editing.

Insert

Switches between Overwrite (OVR) mode, which replaces characters as you type, and Insert mode, which scoots them over to make room for what you type.

##

Moves the cursor one character to the left.

PgDn

Ends editing and moves the cell pointer down 20 rows in the same column.

PgUp

Ends editing and moves the cell pointer up 20 rows in the same column.

Moves the cursor one character to the right.

Shift-Tab

Ends editing and moves the cell pointer one screen to the left in the same row. (Same as Ctrl-←.)

Tab

Ends editing and moves the cell pointer one screen to the right in the same row. (Same as Ctrl-→.)

Ends editing and moves the cell pointer one cell up.

The Dummies Guide to 1-2-3 MENU Mode Keys

End

Moves the highlight to the last menu selection.

Home

Moves the highlight to the first menu selection.

Moves the highlight to the previous menu selection to the left (or wraps around to the last if you're on the first menu choice).

Moves the highlight to the next menu selection to the right (or wraps around to the first if you're on the last menu choice).

You can find more information in Chapters 1 and 2 of *1-2-3 For Dummies*.

Part VII:
The Dummies Guide to
1-2-3 SmartIcons

The 1-2-3 SmartIcons are your mouse's best friend. When you attach the Icons add-in, you see illustrations on the right side of your worksheet. If you have Wysiwyg attached, the pictures are prettier and each one looks like it's on a button. Each SmartIcon represents — and activates — a 1-2-3 command.

This section shows you all 77 of the pretty and not-as-pretty SmartIcons in one big table. In 1-2-3, however, you will find the icons grouped in palettes, or sets, which you can switch among by clicking on the ← and → arrows on each side of the number at the bottom of the palette.

You can lots more information on using the SmartIcons in Chapter 11 of *1-2-3 For Dummies*.

The SmartIcons

Icon in Graphics Mode (Wysiwyg Is Attached)	Icon in Text Mode (Wysiwyg Is Not Attached)	What the Icon Does
	»	Saves a worksheet file.
U	U —	Adds or removes single underlining from the selected range (Wysiwyg must be attached).
U	U =	Adds or removes double underlining from the selected range (Wysiwyg must be attached).
$	$	Formats the values in the selected range with the Currency number format with two decimal places.
0,0	0,0	Formats the values in the selected range with the Comma number format with zero decimal places.
%	%	Formats the values in the selected range with the Percent number format with two decimal places.
AA	2→2	Displays the data in the selected range in the next font in the current font library (Wysiwyg must be attached).
AA	FGRD	Displays the data in the selected range in the next available color (Wysiwyg must be attached).
AA	BGRD	Displays the background of the selected range in the next available color (Wysiwyg must be attached).

(continues)

The SmartIcons *(continued)*

Icon in Graphics Mode (Wysiwyg Is Attached)	Icon in Text Mode (Wysiwyg Is Not Attached)	What the Icon Does
⬜	⬜	Draws an outline and adds a drop shadow to the selected range or removes an existing drop shadow (Wysiwyg must be attached).
⬜	⬜	Draws an outline around the selected range; cycles through all the outline choices: single, double, wide, or clear (Wysiwyg must be attached).
▦	###	Shades the selected range; cycles through shading: light, dark, solid, or clear (Wysiwyg must be attached).
☰	←L	Left-aligns labels in the selected range.
☰	←C→	Centers labels in the selected range.
☰	R→	Right-aligns labels in the selected range.
▦	ALGN TEXT	Centers text across selected columns.
▦	+ROW	Inserts one or more rows above the selected range.
▥	+COL	Inserts one or more columns to the left of the selected range.
▦	−ROW	Deletes the rows in the selected range.
▦	−COL	Deletes the columns in the selected range.

(continues)

The SmartIcons *(continued)*

Icon in Graphics Mode (Wysiwyg Is Attached)	Icon in Text Mode (Wysiwyg Is Not Attached)	What the Icon Does
	— — —	Inserts a horizontal page break in the row with the cell pointer.
	|⋮|	Inserts a vertical page break in the column with the cell pointer (Wysiwyg must be attached).
	A→Z	Sorts the database in ascending (A–Z) order, using the selected column as the sort key.
	Z→A	Sorts the database in descending (Z-A) order, using the selected column as the sort key.
	FILL	Fills the selected range with a series of values, using the Start, Step, and Stop values assigned to /Data Fill (0, 1, and 8191 unless changed).
	CALC	Recalculates all formulas in the worksheet (the same as pressing the F9 [Calc] key).
	DATE	Inserts today's date in the current cell and formats it with the Long International format.
	CRCL	Draws a circle around the selected range (Wysiwyg must be attached).
	ZOOM	Zooms the worksheet display by cycling through the zoom options: Tiny, Small, Normal, Large, and Huge (Wysiwyg must be attached).

(continues)

The SmartIcons *(continued)*

Icon in Graphics Mode (Wysiwyg Is Attached)	Icon in Text Mode (Wysiwyg Is Not Attached)	What the Icon Does
🚶	STEP	Turns on STEP mode to execute a macro one step at a time.
🏃	RUN	Runs the macro of your choice.
←	◄	Moves the cell pointer one cell to the left.
→	►	Moves the cell pointer one cell to the right.
↑	▲	Moves the cell pointer one cell up.
↓	▼	Moves the cell pointer one cell down.
?	?	Displays the 1-2-3 Main Help Index from READY mode.
⌐	⌐	Moves the cell pointer to cell A1, like pressing Home.
⌐	⌐	Moves the cell pointer to the last cell in the active area, like pressing End, Home.
▒↓	‖↓ =	Moves the cell pointer to the first occupied cell below in the same column that is either preceded or followed by a blank cell, like pressing End, ↓.
▒↑	= ‖↑	Moves the cell pointer to the first occupied cell above in the same column that is either followed or preceded by a blank cell, like pressing End, ↑.

(continues)

The SmartIcons *(continued)*

Icon in Graphics Mode (Wysiwyg Is Attached)	Icon in Text Mode (Wysiwyg Is Not Attached)	What the Icon Does
	→ == =	Moves the cell pointer to the first occupied cell to the right in the same row that is either preceded or followed by a blank cell, like pressing End, →.
	== == ←	Moves the cell pointer to the first occupied cell to the left in the same row that is either followed or preceded by a blank cell, like pressing End, ←.
	GOTO	Enables you to select the address or cell range to move the cell pointer to, like pressing the F5 (GoTo) key.
	FIND	Enables you to find or replace a text string in the worksheet, like choosing the /**R**ange **S**earch command.
	UNDO	Undoes your latest goof-up, like pressing the Alt-F4 (Undo) key.
	DEL	Erases the contents of the selected range, like choosing the /**R**ange **E**rase command
	⎡▪⎤»	Retrieves a worksheet file.
⎡+½⎤ ⎣ 3 ⎦	1+2=	Sums values in a selected cell range in empty cells below or to the right of the range, or, if the selected cell range is blank, sums the nearest range of values and places the sums in the empty range.

(continues)

The SmartIcons *(continued)*

Icon in Graphics Mode (Wysiwyg Is Attached)	Icon in Text Mode (Wysiwyg Is Not Attached)	What the Icon Does
		Graphs the values in the selected cell range or the values in the worksheet area surrounding the cell pointer if no range is selected.
		Adds the current graph to the selected range (Wysiwyg must be attached).
	VIEW GRPH	Displays the current graph, like pressing the F10 (Graph) key.
	EDIT TEXT	Enables you to edit a selected text range right in the worksheet itself (Wysiwyg must be attached).
	PRN	Prints the selected range, or, if no range is selected, the print range defined with the 1-2-3 /**Print Printer Range** or the Wysiwyg :**Print Range Set** command.
	PVU	Displays the selected range in the Print Preview screen, or, if no range is selected, the print range defined with the 1-2-3 /**Print Printer Range** or the Wysiwyg :**Print Range Set** command (Wysiwyg must be attached).
	COPY	Copies the selected range when you select the Copy To range.
	MOVE	Moves the selected range when you select the Move To range.

(continues)

The SmartIcons *(continued)*

Icon in Graphics Mode (Wysiwyg Is Attached)	Icon in Text Mode (Wysiwyg Is Not Attached)	What the Icon Does
	COPY FRMT	Copies just the Wysiwyg formatting from the selected range to the new range that you specify.
	REP DATA	Copies the contents of the current cell to all the other cells in the selected range.
B	B	Adds or removes bold typeface from the selected range (Wysiwyg must be attached).
I	í	Adds or removes italics from the selected range (Wysiwyg must be attached).
N	N	Clears all Wysiwyg formatting from the selected range and restores the default font (Wysiwyg must be attached).
		Adds an icon to the custom icon palette.
		Removes an icon from the custom icon palette.
		Enables you to move an icon to a new position in the custom icon palette.
	U	Enables you to assign macros to the 12 User Icons, U1 through U12.

You can find more information on using the SmartIcons in Chapter 11 of *1-2-3 For Dummies*.

Index

Symbols